T0348682

MARKET
SHIFT

MARKET
SHIFT

7 Essential Things to Know About
Real Estate Right Now

Aprile Osborne
Co-Founder of Call it Closed®

Published by RESULTS Faster! Publishing in Flower Mound, TX

Editing by Nonie Jobe

Content Development by Ella Imrie

Cover Design by Bryleigh Andrews

Printed in the United States of America

CONTENTS

FOREWORD

Aprile came into my life several years ago through a referral from a close friend. When I first spoke with her and her husband Chad—co-founders of Call It Closed® (CIC), one of America's fastest-growing real estate brokerages—I could immediately sense their energy, vision, and deep industry knowledge. CIC operates on a cutting-edge model that offers 100 percent commission to its agents, a concept that is reshaping the future of real estate.

I immediately took a liking to Aprile, with her energy, knowledge, and all-around vibe; and I invited both her and Chad to join me in my Dallas-based RESULTS Center. They flew in, as many do, to discuss the clarity of their vision and how I might help them focus and execute that vision. I was impressed as I got to know them both better and understood their history and their passion for helping all stakeholders in residential real estate.

Over the last two decades, I've observed and participated in major industry shifts. I watched as Keller Williams® forever changed real estate by paying people to recruit and then as eXp® founder Glenn Sanford super-scaled his revenue-share-model brokerage while I was coaching and advising him. I recognize when something is set to disrupt the market. What Aprile and Chad have built with CIC is a game-changer. I'm thrilled to be a part of their journey—watching them, strategizing with them, and helping them take their model to the world and strategically grow it while attracting those smart early-adopters who might have missed out on the benefits of the earlier successful models.

As a testament to their success, CIC was recently recognized by *Inc.* magazine as one of the fastest-growing companies in America. And with their plans to go public in the near future, they are on an exciting trajectory that will once again change the real estate industry forever.

Aprile is a very smart real estate all-star, and this book is full of wisdom. While it's written primarily for agents, it also offers valuable insights for brokers, real estate investors, and even homeowners. She introduces powerful concepts like *Realtor IQ*; the "Pajama Effect"; and, most importantly, her Seven Must-Knows, all of which provide clarity and direction in today's shifting real estate landscape.

The real estate market is evolving, and understanding how to navigate these changes can make all the difference. The time you invest in this book is exactly that—an investment. You'll gain insights that will help you make smarter decisions and win more in your real estate career. And do us both a favor—share it with others. Recommend it to fellow agents, investors, and homeowners, and tell them about CIC. In today's world, friends help friends stay ahead—and this book is a roadmap to doing just that.

Tony Jeary - The RESULTS Guy™

INTRODUCTION

THE REAL ESTATE LANDSCAPE IS CHANGING–ARE YOU READY?

The real estate industry is shifting, and it's happening faster than ever before. Markets are evolving, technology is disrupting traditional methods, and consumer expectations are at an all-time high. What worked yesterday won't necessarily work tomorrow, and those who fail to adapt will struggle. Those who respond to these changes in a timely and positive way are winning, and winning big. If you want to be among them—whether you are an agent, a broker, a real estate investor, or even a homeowner—you need to know how to navigate in this dramatic shift.

I'm Aprile Osborne, founder of Call It Closed® and a frequent guest on ABC, Fox, and NBC news affiliates. With over $700 million in career sales, I'm a top-producing real estate expert, a certified Luxury Home Marketing Specialist, and a Million-Dollar-Guild Elite Designee. As a former RE/MAX® speaker and co-owner of the fastest-growing RE/MAX® at that time, I've trained top agents nationwide on how to excel in a rapidly shifting market, helping agents, buyers, and sellers alike understand how to stay ahead of change rather than be overwhelmed by it. What I've learned is that success in real estate has little to do with luck and everything to do with adaptability. This book isn't just about surviving a shifting market—it's about winning in it.

Technology has completely transformed how real estate operates, and it continues to evolve at an astonishing pace. Zillow now pays cash for homes based on its Zestimate, while Google Earth allows buyers to tour entire neighborhoods virtually before they ever step foot in them. AI and blockchain are changing the way transactions are executed, reducing friction and increasing speed. More buyers and sellers are turning to online platforms for property searches, negotiations, and even digital closings. The role of the real estate agent has changed forever. If all you're doing is providing access to listings and handling paperwork, you're already on the way to being replaced. Clients today have unlimited access to information, and they expect more than just a middleman. They need a trusted advisor—someone who understands the data, interprets market trends, and provides insights they can't get on their own.

There is a huge wave of agents moving toward a 100-percent commission model with their brokers. And there is an increasingly larger percentage of realtors who are waking up to the fact that they have been living in a transactional world of huffing and puffing every month— month by month—to keep their hamster wheel going. They now understand they can change their thinking and their efforts to leverage their skill and expertise to make money in their sleep. This book is about these changes and more— where we've been as an industry, where we are, and where we're going. It's not hard to see that the real estate industry is shifting for those who touch it in any way—including realtors and brokers, real estate investors, and homeowners.

Adapting to Thrive in the Market SHIFT

It's not just the world around us that is fluctuating; the consumers in our world are shifting as well. For a real estate agent, a thorough understanding of that shift is imperative. How can you be the best in the business as an industry leader if you don't even know who your consumer is or what they are looking for? Previously, buyers and sellers relied on licensed agents for exclusive market insights, as platforms like Zillow™ and Redfin™ didn't exist. Now, consumers can access property histories and market trends with just a few clicks, reducing their dependence on real estate professionals.

We're dealing with the most knowledgeable consumer in the history of real estate.

It's important to understand that we're dealing with the most knowledgeable consumer in the history of real estate. And because they're more knowledgeable, they're more demanding; and they're moving toward the people who bring professionalism to the table as commissions are being negotiated. The more value you bring to the table, the more you deserve to get paid. People today prefer quality; they prefer fine dining, and they prefer excellent service— which is, of course, what they're wanting for what is typically the most expensive purchase of their lifetime. If you bring value, people will pay for it; if you don't bring value and all you are is a logistics facilitator, they will negotiate your rate.

For example, I have a client who is a very demanding buyer. She and her husband went through several real estate agents before they found me, and I let her critique me all the time and tell me how I could be better as an agent. Obviously, since she's a $15-million buyer, I want to know what she's looking for in an agent. I believe she's basically an expert in the market; and based on what she's been hearing and seen in surveys and personal experience, she believes the IQ of a real estate agent today is really low. And I agree; the agents who actually have what I call a high *Real Estate IQ* are typically more successful. They actively search out things like what school district a home is in or the price of a home per square foot. If you called me today and said, "I want a three-bedroom, two-bath home with a pool, and I want to spend $3 million. What three zip codes can I buy in?" I could just rattle them off to you. That's not true with most real estate agents. So, how do you increase your *Real Estate IQ*? Keep reading, and you'll find out.

Agents who actually have what I call a high Real Estate IQ *are typically more successful.*

Today, many believe agents are less knowledgeable, less professional, and ultimately, less essential than they once were.[1] Consumers are frustrated. Agents don't return calls, they show up unprepared, and they lack the expertise clients expect. It's become

---

1   Ryan Serhant, Forbes, "The 3 Biggest Complaints People Have About Real Estate Agents," April 6, 2021, https://forbes.com (accessed 2/6/2025).

a real issue, and it's affecting the industry's reputation. In fact, often in the viewpoint of the consumer, real estate agents have the same reputation as bad used-car salesmen or attorneys who are just out to steal your money. I jokingly attribute this to what I call "the pajama effect." I watched a documentary recently that talked about the fact that people used to dress up to fly on airplanes, and today they literally wear their pajama pants. Some people may say it's a carryover from so many people working at home and thus becoming a little more lax in the way they dress—regardless, that lack of professionalism has poured over into the way we operate as realtors.

The National Association of Realtors™ reports that unresponsiveness is the top consumer complaint. Studies from Forbes™ and Pinnacle Real Estate Academy highlight issues like dishonesty, misrepresentation, and lack of market knowledge.[2] The reality is that many agents aren't bringing enough value to the table. This presents a massive opportunity. If you commit to professionalism, continuous learning, and excellence in service, you will stand out immediately. The agents who succeed in a shifting market are the ones who take their craft seriously, educate themselves relentlessly, and deliver a level of service that demands respect.

I've designed this book to be a practical, strategic guide for real estate professionals, investors, and homeowners who want to thrive in any market condition. In part one, "Where the Real Estate Industry Has Been," we'll look at the things that used to work in our industry and learn why they don't work today. In

---

2 "The Most Common Complaints Filed Against Real Estate Agents," August 8, 2023, www.pinnaclerealestateacademy.com (accessed 2/6/2025).

part two, "Where the Real Estate Industry is Now," we'll look at the current market environment and emerging trends, and we'll identify gaps in your strategy. In part three, "Where You Want to Be in the Real Estate Industry," we'll show you how to create a winning strategy for current market conditions and how an agent can become a trusted expert in that uncertain market. In "The Path to Getting There," part four, I share seven really valuable "must-knows" for the residential real estate market and give you tips for building relationships that will strengthen your position if you're an agent. I'll also show you how to stay ahead of future market trends. Even though my primary reach for this book is to realtors and brokers, savvy investors and even homeowners can gain valuable insights from the must-knows I offer here.

I invite you to come along with me to see how you can adapt to thrive in the *Market Shift* that's coming. Are you ready?

PART I: WHERE THE REAL ESTATE INDUSTRY HAS BEEN

WHERE THE INDUSTRY HAS BEEN AND HOW IT GOT THERE

I n the 1960s and 1970s, real estate carried a distinct image of professionalism, symbolized by the yellow jacket—a sign of prestige—worn by Century 21 agents.

They set the dress standard for the industry; people noticed and appreciated the professionalism—the class—they represented. Many were immediately drawn to them because their dress identified them as an expert in the real estate field. When I was younger, my uncle owned a real estate company; and he and the other men in the industry wore penny loafers, khaki pants, and a sports jacket every day, while the ladies all wore dresses, They went into the office dressed like professionals, even when they weren't showing a house that day. In fact, people in most industries dressed more professionally.

How you're dressed affects your mindset about how you dominate your day.

So, what happened? When did the real estate agents start mirroring the consumer in their unprofessional "Pajama Effect"? When did they lose the class that was associated with the industry? Of course, the industry has shifted, and we're not going to the office every day. But the truth is, the agent who dresses professionally—as an expert in this business—has the advantage because how you're dressed affects your mindset about how you dominate your day. So it's not just the homeowners or other industry members who react to your dress—it's also you, as a real estate professional. I think the older generation understood that— you dress for the position you want to have. Even if you don't have an appointment that day, you get up and get ready for the day; you command the day. We've seen a loss of that mindset in the industry today.

Real estate is a relationship business, so people look at you in terms of their relationship with you. My uncle understood that, so he would be out there—at the farmer's market, at a restaurant, or wherever—dressed as an expert. So when people looked at him, their first impression was that he was the expert in the industry. I think we need to understand that people are longing for that type of professionalism again.

Back then, the industry operated in an entirely manual way. When I was younger, my uncle owned a real estate company, and I vividly remember how different the business was before the digital age. Without the internet, everything required physical effort. Listing agents had to take photos, print property details, and personally deliver listing pages to every real estate office in town.

For buyers, finding a home was just as labor-intensive. They either visited real estate offices to flip through massive listing books or drove around searching for "For Sale" signs. There was no instant access to market data, filters, or online searches—just endless phone calls and manual inquiries. Brokers also kept unlisted properties in their "hip pocket"—homes that weren't formally recorded yet. Agents would visit a broker's office and ask, "What houses aren't in the system yet?" Deals were often made on the spot, sometimes with properties that hadn't even been publicly listed.

Scheduling a home showing was another logistical challenge. As a buyer's agent, I couldn't simply book an appointment online. Instead, I had to call the listing agent's office on a landline, leave a message, wait for confirmation, drive to the office to pick up the keys, show the home, and return the keys before heading to the next appointment. There were no automated lockboxes, no instant scheduling, and no digital records.

Despite the inefficiencies, this system built stronger relationships between agents and brokers, fostering a deep sense of trust within the industry. The brokerage itself carried weight, as consumers didn't seek out individual agents the way they do today. Instead, they would find a brokerage in the *Yellow Pages*, call the office, and be assigned an agent. The brand name—whether Century 21®, RE/MAX®, or another major brokerage—served as a trusted source of expertise.

The Evolution of Brokerages and Commission Models

In the late 1970s and 1980s, Gary Keller introduced the "pay-to-recruit" model, incentivizing agents to grow brokerages. Later, pioneer Glenn Sanford expanded on this idea with a revenue-sharing model, fundamentally altering how agents could earn beyond their personal sales. Over time, commission structures evolved from traditional 60/40 or 70/30 splits to more agent-friendly models like 80/20, 85/15, and even 100-percent-commission structures.

The introduction of 100-percent-commission models—where agents keep all their earnings but cover their own expenses—disrupted the brokerage-dominated industry. Today, 97 percent of homebuyers start their search online, bypassing the need to connect with a brokerage first. According to the National Association of Realtors (NAR), brokerage branding is no longer a primary factor in a consumer's choice of an agent.

Today, 97 percent of homebuyers start their search online, bypassing the need to connect with a brokerage first.

Instead, consumers choose agents based on one or more of these three key factors:

1. an existing personal relationship;

2. a referral from someone they trust; and/or

3. the agent's (brand or) dominance in the neighborhood or geographical area they're interested in.

By existing personal relationship, I mean someone they have an in-depth relationship with—not just a passing acquaintance. More likely, it would be someone they're close enough to that they would have gone to dinner with them. And when I say people will choose an agent based on a referral from someone they trust, that would be more like a relative or a close friend. Or it could be someone they know and respect in the community.

This is why you need a healthy CRM system to help you maintain your personal relationships. Relationships with people like bankers, brokers, car salesmen, jewelers, art gallery owners, farmers, and other business professionals are so valuable because they have a huge network of people they can refer to you. And they will only give you referrals if they know they can trust you. That's why you need to be very careful what you post on social media. If you're out partying every night and post pictures of that, or even if you're posting about controversial issues like politics, you may lose a lot of the trust people place in you. It could cause someone to have a bad opinion of you and influence them to not give you a referral. Or if you travel a lot and you post about that on social media, people may wonder how they can refer you to someone to sell their house if you're gone all the time. For those reasons, some real estate agents have private Instagram pages that are just for family and friends and a business page for their business world. When you have an Instagram account, there is an invitation process; so you can choose not to approve someone if they are a client.

The Early 2000s Real Estate Boom and Crash

In 2003 and 2004, the housing market saw a massive surge, creating what many saw as an easy path to quick money. Home prices were rising rapidly, and mortgage approvals became incredibly loose—if you had a job and a pulse, you could buy a house with no money down. Investors, flippers, and first-time buyers rushed into the market, taking advantage of easy financing and rising prices.

Real estate agents flooded into the industry, drawn by the prospect of quick commissions. Since homes were selling rapidly, agents could make thousands of dollars per transaction with little effort. Many saw this as an opportunity they couldn't afford to pass up, assuming the housing market would always be this easy.

But few people stopped to consider what would happen if—or, more realistically, *when*—the market slowed down. The assumption was that home values would keep rising indefinitely, allowing buyers to flip properties for a profit before their mortgage payments became unmanageable. This false sense of security led to reckless buying and selling, and many of these new agents never developed the essential skills of negotiation, pricing strategy, or marketing. They didn't have to—it was the easiest sale in the world.

As we now know, it all came crashing down between 2006 and 2008.

What Really Caused the 2006 Market Crash

At the core of the crash was a reckless mortgage system that gave loans to people who couldn't afford them. A major factor was the rise of "no-doc loans" (no documentation loans), which allowed buyers to get approved without proving their income or financial stability.

I remember a story from that era that illustrates how extreme this was. I used to visit a sushi restaurant downtown that had valet parking. One day, the young valet driver, 18 or 19 years old and making $10-$12 an hour, excitedly told me he had just bought two houses to flip in one week with no money down. When I asked how he planned to cover the mortgages if the homes didn't sell immediately, he had no answer. His entire plan relied on flipping them fast.

This was the dangerous mindset fueling the market. Buyers with no financial stability were taking out huge loans. Lenders didn't care because they were packaging these loans and selling them to Wall Street. Appraisers were overvaluing homes to match inflated sale prices, and buyers assumed they could always sell for more before getting stuck with an unaffordable mortgage.

When the market slowed down, homes stopped selling as quickly. Overleveraged buyers—like the valet driver—were now stuck with homes they couldn't afford and couldn't sell.

The Fallout: How the Crash Changed Real Estate Forever

As home values plummeted, foreclosures surged, and banks collapsed, leading to a nationwide financial crisis. The real estate industry took a massive hit, and consumer trust in agents, lenders, and appraisers deteriorated.

Regulations quickly changed to prevent rampant fraud and reckless lending. One of the biggest shifts was in appraiser selection. Previously, real estate agents and lenders could choose appraisers directly, leading to potential conflicts of interest. The new system randomized appraiser selection, ensuring neutrality and preventing inflated home values.

Consumers, now more skeptical than ever, started researching their own real estate data. This shift led to the rise of Zillow and other online platforms, giving buyers and sellers the ability to verify information without relying on agents.

The Lasting Impact of the Housing Crash

Between 2006 and 2009, the real estate market froze, as many buyers feared making a move in an unstable market. However, savvy investors recognized an opportunity. In places like Southwest Florida, homes that once sold for $250,000 dropped to around $50,000 or $60,000. Those who bought at the bottom saw massive returns as the market rebounded.

The 2006 housing crash permanently reshaped the real estate industry. It changed how buyers viewed agents, how transactions were conducted, and how home values were assessed. Today's real estate professionals must work harder than ever to establish trust, provide accurate market insights, and demonstrate value beyond what consumers can find online.

Today's real estate professionals must work harder than ever.

The role of a real estate agent has evolved. In an era where consumers have more information at their fingertips than ever before, only those who bring true expertise, marketing savvy, and negotiation skills will continue to thrive.

PART II: WHERE THE REAL ESTATE INDUSTRY IS NOW

WHERE WE ARE: THE INFORMED CONSUMER AND THE CHANGING REAL ESTATE MARKET

We are in a pivotal moment in history—a moment that isn't just another market cycle but a true hinge year. Unlike a bridge that we cross back and forth, a hinge swings the door in a new direction, opening up new possibilities while closing others.

In this analogy, the trick is knowing which way the door will swing, and even knowing whether you're standing in the right door frame. If you're not in the right brokerage, you could be in the wrong door frame completely; and you may never know which way the door is swinging. You're in the wrong house, and they don't even know there's a door swinging! It's time to get back into the right house.

Right now, several major factors are creating this hinge effect:

1. The economy is shifting. In some places right now, people are dealing with the fact that eggs are $10 a dozen, which is absurd! However, gas has gone down about a dollar, and we want to see those inflationary numbers to continue coming down.

2. Geopolitical tensions, including the possibility of war and trade wars, are impacting market confidence. I'm sensing that more people have confidence that our current administration is more capable of dealing with a war than the last administration was, but obviously no one wants to go to war. As for trade wars, I believe most Americans realize there is a need for them because our trade deficit is partly to blame for causing our inflation number to go up. But I also believe there's an uncertainty about them because

people don't completely understand them. We've not had trade wars in many years; in fact, I don't even remember the last time any politician has gone after these things. I just feel like they are important to bring stability to the economy.

3. Climate-related events and natural disasters are influencing migration patterns. Climate-related matters have always been with us and always will be. The climate is always changing; and yes, weather events do influence where people want to live.

4. Each of these factors is shaping how people buy, sell, and invest in real estate.

5. Consumer confidence is improving, and the market is shifting.

6. Consumer behavior is already responding to these economic changes. I recently spoke with a Mercedes dealership manager just days after the 2024 election. Over the summer, they were preparing to lay off employees due to slow sales. But within three days of the election results, they were selling out of inventory, with buyers suddenly feeling comfortable making large financial decisions again.

The real estate market operates in a similar way. Buyers and sellers are influenced by their confidence in the economy; and when people feel more financially secure, they take action—whether that means upgrading their home, investing in property, or finally listing a home they've been holding onto.

The stock market has already reflected this renewed sense of economic optimism, and real estate will likely follow suit. People are looking at the long term, reassessing their investments, and making decisions based on where they see financial stability returning.

We will never go back to a time before digital listings.

It's important to understand that while consumer confidence is rebounding, we are not returning to the old market. We will never go back to a time before digital listings, before Zillow, or before data-driven decision-making. Just like Amazon changed retail forever, real estate has evolved beyond the days of a black book of listings and a Rolodex of contacts.

The Impact of Short-Term Rentals on Local Communities

The rise of Airbnb and VRBO has fundamentally changed the housing market. What started as a convenient alternative to hotels has now become a major force in real estate, creating both opportunities and challenges. Investors have flocked to short-term rental properties, but their growing presence has shifted market dynamics, often at the expense of local homebuyers.

In many areas, locals are being priced out of their own communities because investors are outbidding them on properties, not as homes, but as income-producing assets. A first-time homebuyer looking for their dream home is now competing with an investor who isn't emotionally attached—just looking at the numbers and willing to pay more if the rental return makes sense.

In many areas, locals are being priced out of their own communities because investors are outbidding them on properties.

Some neighborhoods have responded by restricting short-term rentals—limiting how often a home can be rented out each year or requiring minimum rental periods (such as thirty-day stays). This protects residential communities from turning into mini hotel districts, but it also makes it more difficult for investors to enter certain markets.

For buyers, this means understanding the rules and regulations in different areas is critical. If short-term rentals are allowed with few restrictions, a neighborhood may experience more noise, parties, and transient traffic—a dealbreaker for families looking for stability. On the flip side, if an investor is purchasing a property specifically for Airbnb, they need an expert who understands which areas allow rentals and which ones have restrictions.

This is just another example of how real estate is evolving. The market continues to shift, and successful agents must stay ahead of these trends to properly advise both homebuyers and investors.

Why Sellers Are Less Satisfied Than Buyers

There is a noticeable difference between buyer and seller satisfaction in real estate transactions. Statistics show that buyers report higher satisfaction levels, while only 68 percent of sellers are "very satisfied" with their agent, and 22 percent are only "somewhat satisfied."

The biggest reason? Lack of communication from agents.

Selling a home in today's market requires far more strategy and expertise than it did during the pandemic-era boom, where homes sold in days, often above asking price. Many of the agents who entered the industry during that time never learned true marketing, negotiation, or pricing strategies—they simply listed homes, and they sold. Now that the market has slowed and inventory is sitting much longer, many agents don't know how to adapt.

The national average days on market is now over 200 days in many areas. That's a long time for a seller to wait, especially when agents aren't providing consistent updates. Sellers expect their agent to guide them through the process, adjust the marketing strategy if needed, and be upfront about why a home isn't selling.

Some agents avoid difficult conversations, failing to tell sellers the real reasons their home isn't moving—whether it's overpricing, bad staging, lack of curb appeal, or even an unpleasant smell. Instead of having these honest discussions and repositioning the home correctly, they let it sit, leading to frustration for both sides.

Buyers, on the other hand, are generally more satisfied with their agents because the stakes are lower. While buying a home is still a major decision, buyers are not dealing with the stress of waiting, reducing their price, or adjusting to market conditions the way sellers are.

That said, the importance of long-term relationships in real estate remains clear.

- Eighty-seven percent of sellers said they would "definitely" or "probably" recommend their agent.

- Sixty-six percent of recent sellers used an agent they had worked with before or were referred to by someone they trust.

- Eighty-one percent of sellers contacted only one agent before choosing who to work with.

These statistics reinforce one of the most important truths in real estate: Relationships drive success. The way we connect with buyers and sellers, present homes, and negotiate deals has fundamentally shifted, and those who are waiting for the past to return will be left behind.

Before the housing crash, consumers relied heavily on real estate agents for market insights—past sales, neighborhood values, and pricing trends. But as trust in agents declined, platforms like Zillow stepped in to provide direct access to real estate data. Zillow was among the first to offer past sales history, property photos, and neighborhood price mapping, allowing consumers to research homes independently rather than relying solely on an agent's expertise.

This shift dramatically changed the relationship between agents and their clients. Today, buyers and sellers enter the market better informed than ever before. They scrutinize every move an agent makes; and if they sense a lack of knowledge, they move on. It's not uncommon for a consumer to interview multiple agents before choosing one. One client recently told me she had spoken with twelve different agents before selecting me. That level of scrutiny is the new norm. When people spend hours reading reviews before purchasing something as small as a couch, it makes sense that they would be even more thorough when selecting the person to guide them through one of the largest financial decisions of their lives.

Despite having access to vast amounts of data, many buyers and sellers still need professional guidance.[3] However, the role of the real estate agent has changed. It's no longer enough to simply provide listing information—consumers already have that. The true value of an agent lies in interpreting the market,

3 Stephen Brobeck, Consumer Federation of America, "Choosing a Real Estate Agent: An Evaluation of Information Sources About Quality of Service," July 2020, www.consumerfed.org (accessed 2/6/2025).

understanding the nuances of different neighborhoods, and being able to navigate negotiations effectively. Some agents make the mistake of relying only on raw market data—home prices, price per square foot, and days on market. While those metrics matter, they're only part of the picture. The best agents don't just know the numbers—they understand the lifestyle that comes with each neighborhood.

It's no longer enough to simply provide listing information—consumers already have that.

Some agents argue that they don't need to physically preview neighborhoods, believing online resources like Google Earth provide all the insight they need. But a buyer doesn't just want to know if an area looks nice on a map—they want to feel the neighborhood, experience the streets, and understand the community. That's something an agent can't convey if they've only looked at the area through a screen. The agents who immerse themselves in their markets, exploring communities firsthand, are the ones who gain trust. I've had buyers and sellers ask me, "Do you live in this neighborhood?" simply because of how much I knew about it. My answer?

"I might as well." That level of familiarity builds instant credibility.

The Challenge of Buyer's Brokerage Agreements

With consumers more informed than ever, they're also more aware of commission fees and questioning whether an agent's service is worth the cost. This has become even more pressing with the growing use of buyer's broker agreements, which often require buyers to agree to pay their agent's commission if the seller does not.

Previously, buyers didn't have to think about paying their agent—the seller typically covered the commission. Now, they're signing legal agreements that could make them financially responsible for that payment. If they don't completely trust their agent, why would they willingly commit to spending tens of thousands of dollars in commission fees? This shift is another reason agents can no longer rely on simply showing up. They must demonstrate their value from the first interaction.

I recently showed a home where I required the buyer to sign a buyer's brokerage agreement beforehand. I pointed to the contract and said, "See where it says the amount of commission right there? Don't worry—I'm going to make sure the seller covers that. You won't be paying it." I said it with absolute confidence because I had already proven my expertise. If I hadn't earned their trust beforehand, there's no way they would have signed a document committing to potentially pay thousands of dollars in commission on a million-dollar home.

So the real challenge with the buyer's brokerage agreements is that they demand that those agents who are not really professionals in the field become experts—and that's where we actually find them to be an advantage.

The Rise of Misinformed Consumers

While buyers and sellers today have access to more data, they don't always have accurate data. One of the biggest sources of misinformation in real estate is Zillow's Zestimate. Zillow estimates home values based on broad metrics—square footage, recent sales, and the approximate age of the property—but it fails to account for critical details that can significantly affect a home's true market value.

A house that has undergone $250,000 in upgrades, including a new kitchen, roof, appliances, and flooring, should not be valued the same as a neighboring home with no renovations. However, Zillow's algorithm often ignores these differences, leading to misleading estimates that create unrealistic expectations for buyers and sellers.

Realtors today not only have to educate their clients but also correct false assumptions created by online data. Sellers may believe their home is worth more than it actually is, while buyers may think they're overpaying or getting a steal based on flawed automated valuations. This misinformation complicates pricing negotiations and makes it even more crucial for agents to assert their expertise in market analysis.

The Impact of Market Shifts in Recent History

Another major challenge in today's market is the reluctance of homeowners to sell. Prior to the pandemic, the economy was at an all-time best-case scenario. So obviously people could purchase larger homes during that time because interest rates were 2 and 3 percent. If you do the math on the mortgage rate of a $500,000 house with a 3 percent loan versus a 5 percent loan, of course you see that the monthly payment is much less. So people who normally couldn't afford a $500,000 house before now could. Then the virus appeared, and with it the lockdown.

During the lockdown, there were people sitting in their homes thinking they were going to be locked inside for a year, maybe more. Many of them thought, *This may be our new life. So if we're going to stare at these four walls, we want to do something different with these four walls. We want bigger kitchens, bigger living rooms, a workspace, playrooms, and a homeschool room because our kids are at home.* So that became a driving force for people to move because now they were working from home. There were also people moving who, say, worked in Chicago because that's where their office was; but now that they didn't have to go to the office and could do their job from home, home could be anywhere in the world. So now they were looking at the map of the whole United States asking, *Where do I want to live, since I can live anywhere and still keep my job? Do I want to live in Texas, do I want to live in California,* or *do I want to live in Florida, or wherever?* It was an option that had never been presented before in the history of life. Never before had people been able to work from home and get to choose where that home was.

That was a huge driving force behind the pandemic market. The Census Bureau report revealed that in 2020, 330,000 people left California. It was the largest demographic swing from one state into other states in the history of California. Some people say it was due to political issues; I agree that had a part in it, but I also believe there were other factors: taxes, the cost of living, and the fact that people could get bigger houses for much less money in states like Texas than they had in California.

Never before had people been able to work from home and get to choose where that home was.

Now, of course, we're seeing that business owners want their people coming back to work in their business locations so they can regain the productivity of their employees. And I can speak to that for my business as well. During the lockdown, we obviously had no choice; our staff had to work from home. But we saw their productivity level go down, compared to what it was when they were in the office. I don't think people intentionally worked less; but when you're working from home, the "Pajama Effect" seems to kick in. (We all saw those memes where people were dressed in a business suit from the top up, and they were in their pajamas or less from the waist down.) You're thinking about the laundry, or you might take a nap or do other things you wouldn't do in an office setting. That's why I believe business owners are pushing more to have people back in the office. I don't think it has anything to do with the current administration. We may never again see a time when people have the opportunity to work from home.

If you think about it, the shift was already happening right before the pandemic. The consumers were already more knowledgeable. They had more information at their fingertips than we've ever had in the history of real estate—or in life in general, for that matter. Everyone had started reading reviews and all the details available online prior to shopping, eating at a restaurant, going to a city, moving to a neighborhood, etc.

It was as if the pandemic was the gasoline that started the fire of the market shift. Or, more realistically, It just added fuel to the fire that was already burning. The shift was already in a slow burn; but because of the pandemic, it became a massive burn. People were sitting at home researching the life they wanted to live in this new world of the pandemic, which they thought would be our world for a while, and now we're coming out of that. People are now getting readjusted to outside-of-pandemic numbers.

So did the pandemic play a role in the market shift of today? I would say yes, because it caused people to look at things differently. They started looking at family differently, at school differently, at business differently, at job opportunities differently, and at their lifestyle differently—including what they wanted to do inside their home and outside of their home.

For example, golf course memberships went up across the country by record numbers because people wanted to be outside. They were asking, *What can I do outside that's not going to put me in danger of catching a virus?* So they started playing things like golf, tennis, and pickleball. Overall, they just began to do life differently than they used to. Movie attendance went down because people wanted to be more active outdoors, which I think is incredible. That's part of the blessing of the shift; it has created a more active living style, which will hopefully lead to a healthier lifestyle.

Many who purchased homes during the COVID market secured mortgage rates around 2 to 3 percent, while recent rates have surged to 7 percent or higher. Selling now would mean giving up an incredibly low mortgage payment in exchange for a much higher one, making many homeowners hesitant to move—even if their current home no longer suits them.

Even those who no longer need as much space are holding onto their properties because of the financial advantage of a lower interest rate. I've spoken to many clients who would like to move but ultimately decide against it. One seller told me, "I'm going to keep this house forever because it has a 2 percent interest rate." That may be an exaggeration, but it illustrates the psychological barrier that's keeping many homeowners from listing their homes.

However, what many homeowners fail to realize is that their home equity presents a second wave of opportunity. Even with a higher interest rate, selling now can still be a smart financial move. The equity gained from the sale can serve as a significant down payment on a new home, reducing the impact of higher mortgage rates and, in many cases, keeping monthly payments manageable.

What many homeowners fail to realize is that their home equity presents a second wave of opportunity.

For many, the trade-off isn't just about interest rates—it's about leveraging their financial position to move into a home that better suits their needs, whether that means upgrading, downsizing, or relocating. Holding onto a home solely because of a lower rate may seem like the safest option; but in reality, it could mean missing out on a better overall financial opportunity.

With fewer homes on the market, buyers have limited options, which drives prices up and creates a frustrating environment for those looking to purchase. While life events will eventually force some homeowners to move, many are choosing to wait until interest rates become more favorable.

So how does all this compare to what happened with the market shift that took place in 2006 to 2008? I don't think there's any comparison relating to the way we do life. That shift was economy driven. At that point there was so much hype in what the market was doing. And it wasn't in every market across the country. Everything was going well, but there were pockets that were going extremely well because there was such a driving force of both good interest rates and good economy. Interests rates were around 5 percent—not 2, 3, or 4 percent—but the overall economy was doing fabulous. People were making more money. The unemployment rate was down, at an all-time low. There was just a lot of excitement— and when people are happy, they spend more money. It's like when someone gets married; they will often gain fifteen pounds because they're just so happy. They eat more, and they generally spend more. It's the same with college students—the "freshman fifteen" happens because they are just so happy to be in this new phase of their life.

It's also similar with real estate. Sometimes agents forget what an impact feelings have in this industry; how people feel about a neighborhood, about the economy, or just about certain situations is a driving force in the real estate market shifts. Purchasing property is an emotional event, and I think the emotions of people in the early 2000s before the crash were driving that market.

The Effect of Overspending

These last couple of years, people have been spending a lot; and they are so deeply in debt that they will soon face a reckoning. They got comfortable during the pandemic because everything was so healthy financially; they got used to a certain lifestyle of spending. During the last couple of years, we've not had those same financial wins, but people have not wanted to change their lifestyle to accommodate a new budget; consequently, they've been overspending on credit cards.

Could that cause a problem in our market correction? At some point the gravy train will stop and the debtors will start knocking on their doors, and they will either settle or start doing life differently. I don't believe we will have a crash with a massive load of inventory, but I do believe we will see some foreclosures. At this point, people have high hopes because President Trump is back in office; if you look back at his previous four years, he was successful in facilitating a booming economy. So I think because of that, we may not see as big a foreclosure market as some are expecting.

Some people fear the trade wars and the tariffs may cause lumber or other prices to go up; but the reality is, President Trump is trying to force the suppliers to buy from the United States versus from outside of the country, which will actually help Americans make more money. If you're in the wood-making business, for example, you want suppliers to come to you and not have a company from another nation undercut you. (No pun intended.) So the trade wars and the tariffs are like a double-edged sword—they have their negatives, but they also have their positives.

Why Technology Won't Replace Agents

With companies like Zillow™ and Opendoor™ introducing automated systems such as self-access lockboxes and direct cash offers, some wonder if real estate agents will eventually become obsolete. But these new systems fail to address the complexities, security concerns, and trust issues that come with buying and selling a home.

Zillow and other platforms now offer sellers the option of accepting direct cash offers or using a low-cost service that places a lockbox on their home, allowing potential buyers to access it without an agent. While this may sound convenient, it introduces significant security risks. Some services allow entry simply by submitting a valid driver's license, which means anyone with a license—or even a stolen ID—could gain access to a property.

This creates a massive vulnerability for homeowners. Imagine an empty home being accessed by someone looking for a place to sleep or a group of teenagers using it for a party. Even with restrictions, it only takes minutes for someone to cause damage. Most homeowners are not comfortable allowing unverified strangers into their most valuable asset, which is why these systems have failed to replace traditional agents.

Beyond security, real estate professionals do far more than just open doors. They handle pricing strategy, negotiations, contracts, marketing, and the countless details involved in guiding clients through complex transactions. No app or automated system can replicate the trust, strategic insight, and problem-solving abilities that a skilled agent brings to the table. Again, the level of professionalism of the agent can determine the buyer's or seller's level of confidence in the agent.

The Reality Check for Agents: Adapt or Leave

The real estate industry is evolving, and the agents who treat it as a real business will continue to succeed, while those who entered for quick money are already fading out. During the COVID boom, many new agents—whom we called "order takers"—entered the business, thinking it would always be that easy. They didn't invest in learning marketing, building relationships, or financial planning. When the market slowed, they couldn't sustain themselves and had to return to traditional jobs.

No app or automated system can replicate the trust, strategic insight, and problem-solving abilities that a skilled agent brings to the table.

The real estate agent model isn't dying—it's just weeding out those who never took it seriously. The agents who understand marketing, build strong relationships with lenders and title companies, and adapt to changing market conditions will continue to thrive. Those who rely on outdated methods or refuse to grow will struggle.

Change for the real estate agent is absolutely vital—it can mean the success or failure of your business. Many people struggle with change; they find it difficult to push themselves out of their comfort zones. For example, people often get stuck in specific patterns because, by nature, humans are creatures of habit. We wake up and follow the same routines every morning—whether it's drinking coffee, brushing our teeth, reading a book, working out, or skipping the workout.

Because we are so accustomed to these patterns, breaking them can be extremely challenging. This is especially true in the real estate business, where professionals often fall into repetitive patterns in marketing, community engagement, and client interactions. The problem is that they may be unaware of their blind spots—areas where they are not growing or evolving with the culture.

Staying ahead means keeping up with technological advancements, shifts in consumer behavior, and industry trends. Ask yourself:

- Where are my clients coming from?
- What do they want?
- What kind of agent do I need to be to best serve them?

Be assured, this isn't the end of real estate agents—it's just the end of mediocre ones.

So, to recap:

- One of the biggest risks in real estate—whether you're an agent, broker, or investor—is being unwilling to change with the times.

- For agents, failing to evolve means clinging to outdated marketing tactics, ignoring digital advancements, and failing to recognize the importance of branding. Many agents still operate in a transactional mindset, always chasing the next deal instead of cultivating long-term relationships that generate repeat and referral business.

- For brokers, the biggest vulnerability is sticking to outdated commission splits and structures that no longer work for modern agents. Real estate professionals today demand more flexibility, revenue-sharing opportunities, and long-term wealth-building potential—and brokers who ignore these needs will lose their best agents to forward-thinking firms.

- For investors, the mistake is not diversifying their approach. Relying solely on short-term flips or a single market can be risky, especially in an environment where interest rates, rental regulations, and home values fluctuate rapidly.

- Fear is a business killer in real estate.

- As a buyer, you may be so afraid of market conditions that you stay stuck in analysis paralysis, waiting for the "perfect time" that may never come.

- As a seller, you may be holding onto a low mortgage rate, thinking that selling now is a financial mistake. But if you've built up significant equity, that profit could be leveraged into a new opportunity, even in a higher-rate market. Waiting too long means missing the next wave of appreciation.

- As an agent, you may hesitate to learn new skills, embrace social media, or invest in your brand, fearing change instead of recognizing the competitive advantage it brings.

- In today's market, buyers and sellers are more informed than ever, which means real estate professionals need to level up. It's not enough to blend in with the competition—you have to stand out as a true expert.

- Digital marketing, personal branding, and niche expertise set top-performing agents apart. If you're not using these tools, you risk being just another name in a sea of agents.

- For brokers, if you're not training your agents to become local experts, they won't survive—and neither will your brokerage.

- For investors, relying purely on gut instinct without leveraging big data and predictive analytics means missing profitable opportunities in emerging markets.

- The most successful real estate professionals understand the power of relationships.

- Referrals drive business. Sixty-six percent of sellers work with an agent they have used before or who was referred to them, proving that long-term relationships generate repeat business.

- Networking with other agents nationwide is no longer optional. With so many people relocating, having trusted referral partners in other markets creates additional income streams.

- Brokers who foster a strong community culture keep their best agents, while those who isolate themselves lose agents to firms that provide mentorship, collaboration, and revenue-sharing opportunities.

- Agents who depend solely on commissions are at risk. Real estate is cyclical, and when the market slows, those without additional income streams struggle to survive.

The most successful real estate professionals understand the power of relationships.

- Savvy agents and brokers are now building passive income through rental properties, investment deals, revenue-sharing models, and real estate-related businesses.

- Investors are diversifying beyond traditional flips and rentals, looking into short-term rentals, multi-family investments, and alternative financing opportunities.

- Homeowners should think like investors, considering whether to sell, rent, or leverage their equity rather than simply sitting on their assets.

The Current Market Shift from the Viewpoint of a Mortgage Industry Expert

"The real estate market is undergoing a significant correction rather than a crash," agreed a mortgage industry expert. "Many consumers mistakenly attribute the historically low interest rates of a few years ago to the pandemic, when in reality, rates in the 2 to 3 percent range were already in place before COVID-19. Government intervention, particularly through the subsidization of mortgage-backed securities and the purchase of treasuries, created an artificial environment that drove rates to unsustainable lows.

"As a result, many homeowners are now reluctant to sell, as they are locked into exceptionally low mortgage rates, making higher current rates less attractive for refinancing or new purchases. This phenomenon has led to stagnation in housing inventory, as individuals who might otherwise relocate are choosing to stay put rather than trade their favorable interest rates for higher ones."

"The government didn't step in soon enough to rein in the market when we had 2 percent interest rates," the expert continued. "These ultra-low rates inflated home prices, leading to a situation where many homeowners are now 'stuck.' A significant number of people are hesitant to sell, as they're locked into exceptionally low mortgage rates, making higher current rates less appealing for refinancing or new purchases. This reluctance has created a stagnation in housing inventory, with potential sellers opting to stay put rather than trade their favorable rates for higher ones."

"Interest rates will likely improve as treasury buybacks commence, and housing supply catches up," the mortgage expert continued. "However, the biggest concern is credit card debt. Many consumers extended their lifestyles beyond sustainable means, and without responsible policy measures, we could see financial strain affecting homeownership trends.

Looking ahead, the expert anticipates that the market will begin to recalibrate as interest rates eventually drop. She predicts that 2025 could see a more active market, with sales picking up as rates ease, especially in the latter half of the year. However, the landscape will be different from the past. With rising home prices and consumers feeling the impact of higher costs, the demand will be more cautious, but still strong enough to signal recovery. The market will likely stabilize as buyers and sellers adjust their expectations to a more realistic set of market conditions.

PART III: WHERE YOU AS A REAL ESTATE PROFESSIONAL WANT TO BE

WHERE YOU WANT TO BE IN THE REAL ESTATE INDUSTRY

Why Traditional Marketing Strategies Are Losing Effectiveness

Old-school real estate marketing—cold calls, mailers, and door-knocking—doesn't work the way it used to. While some of these methods still have a place in certain markets, the way consumers interact with marketing has shifted dramatically.

Take door-knocking, for example. Decades ago, it was common for people to welcome unexpected visitors, even inviting them in for a chat. Today, most people are skeptical of unannounced knocks on their door. There's even a joke about how in the 1970s, if someone knocked, families would rush to the door, excited to see who was visiting. Today, if someone knocks, people turn off the lights, tell the kids to be quiet, and pretend they aren't home. That cultural shift makes door-knocking far less effective.

Cold calling has also evolved. I personally don't like to call it cold calling—I prefer to think of it as warm calling. If a homeowner has listed their property as "For Sale By Owner" or their listing has recently expired, they have already expressed an interest in selling. That means they are actively inviting conversations about real estate. Calling them to offer your services isn't the same as randomly reaching out to people who haven't expressed any interest in moving.

However, agents face another challenge—competition. Many of the same leads are receiving calls from multiple agents. By the time you reach them, they may have already heard from ten other agents, leading to frustration and resistance. That's why the best strategy isn't to chase the freshest leads—it's to go after the ones that most agents have already forgotten about.

For example, instead of calling a brand-new expired listing, try reaching out to a property that expired six months ago but never relisted. Those homeowners may still want to sell but have given up after a poor experience. Since most agents aren't calling them anymore, they are often more receptive to a conversation.

Real estate marketing is evolving, and the agents who succeed are the ones who understand these shifts and adjust their strategies accordingly. It's not about abandoning traditional methods entirely, but about using them in smarter, more effective ways that align with today's consumer behavior.

Predicting Future Shifts

This is a massive topic that goes beyond just real estate. To anticipate changes in the mortgage market, it's crucial to observe trends in other industries. For example, before the real estate market exploded during the COVID era, we saw a surge in demand for luxury items. Rolex watches became harder to get, high-end cars were selling out, and even luxury boats were difficult to purchase. There was an undeniable trend of buyers spending aggressively in a hot and healthy market.

Another key indicator is the movement of gold prices. When economic uncertainty rises, gold purchases tend to increase, signaling shifts in financial markets that often align with changes in real estate and mortgage trends.

One of the most challenging yet essential topics in market forecasting is understanding the influence of government policies and global events on consumer confidence. While this can be a sensitive subject, the reality is that government stability—or instability—has a direct impact on the real estate market and broader investment behavior.

One of the most challenging yet essential topics in market forecasting is understanding the influence of government policies and global events on consumer confidence.

For example, when there are rumors of war, geopolitical conflicts, or economic uncertainty, buyers tend to hesitate. They may hold off on purchasing additional investment properties or second homes, or even delay homeownership altogether, opting to continue renting instead. This hesitation is driven by a lack of confidence in the market, stemming from larger concerns about government leadership, inflation, interest rates, and national stability.

History has proven this pattern time and time again.
If you look back at the Jimmy Carter era, for instance,
mortgage interest rates were around 18-21 percent, yet
people were still buying homes. However, the way they
bought, moved, and invested shifted dramatically in response
to the economic climate. Similarly, when the overall economy
is unsettled, you'll notice a ripple effect across multiple
industries—luxury goods, real estate, art, watches, boats,
high-end jewelry, and automobiles all experience parallel ups
and downs.

When the government is at unrest, the economy is at unrest;
and in turn, the market follows suit. We see these patterns play out
in real time, and they are critical indicators for staying ahead of
economic shifts.

This is why it's so important to stay informed—not just about
real estate trends, but about legislation, economic policies, global
conflicts, and governmental decision-making. These elements
influence consumer confidence, which in turn shapes market
movements long before they hit the headlines.

The market itself gives pretty strong clues as well. In 2006, I
had one house that I sold to seven different investors, one right
after another, with no one ever moving into in the home. Each
investor made anywhere from $20 to $40,000 from their sale.
Because the market was moving at such a fast pace, it would go
up $10,000 one month, $20,000 the next, and maybe another
$20,000 the next. An investor would think, *I just bought this
house last month, but I can make $20,000 if I sell it now, so why
not?*

Well, I firmly believe a house is meant to be lived in, not just
be flipped; and I started feeling like someday someone had to

move into that house. We couldn't just keep selling it for $20 to
$30,000 more each time. So that was the first thing that began to
pique my interest. I was wondering, *When are they actually going
to rent the house out? Where is the family that is going to live here?*
Because of who I am, that's the way I think. The house was not
anyone's home—it had just turned into an investor feeding frenzy,
like *Shark Tank*.

The house was just going from one investor to another to
another; so from that perspective, I don't blame the mortgage
people 100 percent for that crash, I don't think it was the
mortgage brokers' fault; I believe it was mostly the fault of the
lending institutions that were offering the loans to basically
anyone. It was almost to the point that if you were eighteen
or older, had a pulse, and could show you had a job, you could
buy a house. It was literally the wildest thing I had ever seen.
And that kind of lending craziness was just creating more
investors—non-certified investors who were coming to the
market and just purchasing over and over. It was driving the
fish tank of investors to an all-time high, and I began to feel the
pressure.

Remember my story about the twenty-year-old valet driver in
Naples who was making $12 an hour and had no savings, but he
had been able to buy two homes to flip with a no-money-down
loan? That was the tipping point for me. I said, "There's no way
we can sustain this." So the next morning I got up and started
calling 355 investors and said, "We have to sell. A crash is coming.
This market is not sustainable." When I had sold one house seven
times to seven different investors and no one had ever moved into
that house, I knew a crash was coming; I felt it before anyone else
in my market did. Some of the agents who worked at the company

I was with literally thought I had lost my mind. I kept saying, "No, the market is crashing!" That was in the middle of 2006. I told every one of my investors to liquidate, and they all did except two—and those two investors both lost over a million dollars in the market.

That's why I know we're not in a crash today; we're in a correction. I know it's not a crash because It's not the investors who are circling; it's the buyers. They are waiting to buy because they're waiting for the interest rates to go down. That's a total different correction in the market—one that's being driven by people who are waiting to feel more comfortable before they buy. Remember, it's all about the emotion for the buyer.

The key is that, as a real estate agent, you can't be influenced by your emotions. You have to look at what's happening on paper—two plus two have to equal four. No matter how pretty the two is or how fancy the four is, it still has to equal. So many agents go by their emotions. They *feel like* something is happening, and that's not always the case. It's such a crazy dichotomy, because it's often all emotion on the buyer's end, but nothing on the agent's end can be based on emotion. My dad used to say, "The deal's not done until the taillights hit the street." When the deal is done, that's when you can give in to the emotions; but you don't allow the emotions during the game.

As far as that crash goes, I do think there were warnings along the way that other people saw—I just didn't know who those people were. I think most realtors were too busy to notice because of the sheer volume of sales they were experiencing. At one point, I had a line in my office of thirty people who were waiting to see me to write contracts. I was writing them so fast there wasn't time to breathe or think. So I don't want to blame the agents, because there just wasn't enough time to do due diligence. I believe the reason I felt it is because I got into a bubble of 77 lobbyist investors out of Washington, D.C. And when I saw them passing around properties to each other for a profit, that was weird to me. Other agents didn't have that same opportunity to see it as closely as I was able to.

The key is that, as a real estate agent, you can't be influenced by your emotions.

And again, I think I took note because family and home are at my heart's core. I kept looking for the family. Most agents don't think that way, unfortunately. They're usually thinking about how they can make more money or how they can be the most successful real estate agent in the business. When I broke the record of 355 homes in eight months, I didn't even know there was a record to be broken. I wasn't even counting my deals. It was just that I love the business so much, and I was actually thinking each time about the person sitting in front of me.

I think that plus the advantages I had with the people I was running with are why I saw it coming. It's so important who you keep closest to you in this business. It's a good reason for you to want to be next to leaders. That's why here at Call It Closed we have brought the biggest leaders to the table, And that's why it took so long to do what we're doing today, because I didn't have access to them—and now I do. We want our agents to be very informed. I don't believe a lot of brokers and owners and leaders in the industry have any clue about what's going on in the market, really, because they're so disconnected from the field.

It' so important for homeowners and investors to choose an agent who is surrounded by the most intelligent and knowledgeable leaders in the industry. Really, why would they select an agent who is not surrounded by the right mentors and the right coaches? Most homeowners don't even think about that. I actually think who we're being coached and trained by should be a part of our listing presentation, because that's a missing piece for homeowners. That's how their agents are going to stay ahead of the game when they're getting consumers into the front door of that house. It's so beautiful when you're interviewing a real estate agent to see that they're surrounded by the heaviest mentors. That's why here at Call It Closed we've surrounded our agents with the best of the best—like Tony Jeary, Hoss Pratt, Robbie Page, and Eric Golden and others, who are among the most forward-thinking trainers and coaches in the business.

To this day, I think about that sushi valet kid; I wish I knew where he is in life today. Since that happened right at the tail end of that market, just before the crash began, I doubt he ever sold those houses for what he paid for them. He was probably foreclosed on. He should never have even been given the option to get that loan at such a young age. I feel sorry for people like that; they don't know because they have no life experience. He had no idea how to choose a knowledgeable, experienced agent. If I had been his agent, I would at least have said, "You're not buying two; let's just buy one." So I do blame the realtor, and even the mortgage person who did the loan, for part of that. There was a level of greed driving that deal. They had no clue about the market, and they obviously had no compassion for him.

Developing Resilience and Adaptability for Market Shifts

Most real estate agents today operate with a transactional mindset, constantly chasing the next deal. While securing new business is important, focusing solely on the next sale causes agents to overlook the long-term potential of the clients standing right in front of them. I had a client who referred me to ten or more family members—brothers, aunts, and children, and even their parents' investment properties. That one initial transaction became a lifelong source of repeat business because I prioritized relationships over transactions.

Agents who fail to shift their mindset toward relationship-based selling will struggle to build a lasting career. Even in today's data-driven, technology-heavy culture, people still crave personal connection. They want to be seen, heard, and valued. If an agent treats them as nothing more than another commission check, they will take their business elsewhere. Real estate isn't just about selling homes—it's about guiding people through one of the biggest financial and emotional decisions of their lives. Clients want an agent who listens to their needs, values their desires, and provides long-term value—not just someone who rushes them through a deal.

Without long-term relationships, there is no long-term business. Real estate isn't just about closing a deal today; it's about building trust, staying relevant, and becoming the go-to resource for years to come. A successful career in this industry requires more than just a focus on buyers and sellers—it also depends on strong connections with lenders, title companies, attorneys, appraisers, and inspection companies. A well-connected agent isn't just someone who sells homes; they are a trusted advisor who can provide clients with the best resources every step of the way.

Without long-term relationships, there is no long-term business.

In the home-buying process, it starts with the realtor; you are the buyer's primary point of contact. So just like you would refer them to a different realtor if they were moving out of state, you're referring them to lenders, attorneys, title companies, etc. when they move into your community; so you want to make sure you're recommending the best.

At Call It Closed, we have relationships with different people as a company; but we train our agents to vet these vendors themselves and go after the best in their local market because each market is different. So after you vet them, you want to build relationships with them. It's a personal thing, so there's no way the company can do that for you. My personal choice might not be your favorite person.

Beyond industry relationships, forming connections with local business owners is equally valuable. Pet groomers, restaurants, nail salons, and hairstylists all play a role in a client's life, especially if they are moving to a new part of town. When a client relocates, they aren't just looking for a house; they are looking for a community. Being able to provide trusted recommendations for local businesses adds another level of value to the agent-client relationship. These relationships also work both ways—when agents refer business to local vendors, those vendors often return the favor, creating a mutually beneficial network.

Statistics from the National Association of Realtors support the importance of this approach. Fifty-nine percent of buyers say the quality of the neighborhood was the top factor in their decision, while 45 percent said proximity to friends and family influenced their choice. Eighty-eight percent of homebuyers purchased their home through a real estate agent or broker, with nearly half of buyers seeking help finding the

right home and another 14 percent wanting assistance with
negotiations.

Understanding these numbers reinforces why an agent
must be more than just a salesperson. A deep knowledge of the
neighborhood, local amenities, and market trends helps position
an agent as the expert buyers are looking for. While an agent can't
control where a client's friends and family live, they can become
the person who knows everything about the area they're moving
to. Buyers want more than someone who can unlock doors—they
want someone who understands the lifestyle that comes with the
home they're purchasing.

Negotiation skills are also a critical part of an agent's value.
As we've said, buying a home is an emotional process, and that
emotion can cloud a buyer's judgment. Even as a top negotiator,
I would rather have someone else negotiate for me if I were
purchasing my own home. It's too easy to make emotional
decisions, to overpay, or to accept terms that aren't in my best
interest.

I once had a client looking at a home listed at $1,150,000.
She wanted to offer full price in cash with a 15-day closing,
fearing the home would sell quickly. But based on my market
knowledge, I knew the market was starting to slow. I assured
her that I could save her $50,000 and suggested we offer
$100,000 below asking to see how the seller responded. She
hesitated, worried about losing the home, and even told me, "If
you lose this house, you're fired." I welcomed the challenge. In
the end, the seller countered, and we closed at $50,000 under
asking. Had my client acted on emotion alone, she would have
overpaid. Instead, by trusting my expertise, she walked away
with a significant savings.

The best real estate agents are not just focused on transactions. They build lasting relationships, establish themselves as community experts, and understand the importance of negotiation. An agent who invests in relationships will always have a steady stream of repeat business. A broker who encourages this approach will retain top-performing agents. A buyer or seller who works with an agent who prioritizes long-term value will make better financial decisions.

> *An agent who invests in relationships will always have a steady stream of repeat business.*

Increasing Your Value by Increasing Your *Real Estate IQ*

I mentioned that the most successful agents have what I call a high *Real Estate IQ*. Part of your *Real Estate IQ* is knowing your brand and having a high level of awareness of who you are as an agent. You can't be insecure; you must be confident, which is why it's so important to be an expert.

The first question you must ask yourself is: What am I an expert in?

Are you an expert in:

- Land and farmland?
- Golf course communities?
- Beach communities?
- New developments or working with builders?
- Single-family homes?
- Condos, including golf course condos or riverfront condos?

- The list goes on.

But before you claim expertise, ask yourself: *Can I confidently justify it?*

The definition of an expert is someone who has studied and mastered a particular subject. If you have only surface-level knowledge of multiple areas but aren't truly proficient in one, you may struggle to stand out. The biggest mistake many agents make is trying to be everything to everyone, spreading themselves too thin. You don't have to limit yourself to just one specialty forever. However, start by mastering one niche before branching out.

For example, if you choose golf course communities, true expertise means knowing details like:

- The locations and reputations of all golf courses in your market
- The designers of each course
- Membership costs and tiers
- Whether membership is included in the home purchase

- The presence of a golf pro and the cost of lessons
- Tee time availability and booking processes
- Driving range length and difficulty levels

A client may come to you saying, "I want to buy in a golf course community, with a $550,000 budget, a maximum $100,000 golf membership fee, and easy course access. I also want a Jack Nicklaus-designed course with an on-staff pro. Where can I find that?"

If you can't answer that immediately, you aren't a golf course community expert.

The same logic applies to other real estate niches—whether it's pickleball communities, beachfront properties, or luxury developments. The goal is to build a high *Real Estate IQ* in your specialty.

I find that people are insecure when they don't know something. *Knowledge is power.* When you have a high level of knowledge about something and can speak intelligently about it, you're more confident. If you can't speak intelligently about it, your insecurity shows. You definitely don't want to be a person in this business who doesn't know what you're talking about, and you don't want to be fumbling around trying to find information or just rambling off something.

Another part of being an expert is looking the part. You have to look at yourself and ask:

- *What does my look say?*
- *Do I look like I'm an expert?*
- *Do I look like I know what I'm talking about?*

It's extremely important to understand that people judge you within just a few seconds of meeting you by the way you look. They are forming an opinion about you from the moment they lay eyes on you, before you even open your mouth. So do you look like a real estate expert or do you look like a golfer or an unprofessional person? That's part of the "Pajama Effect" I've been talking about. Do you look like you just rolled out a bed or like you're selling something besides real estate? If you want to be taken seriously as an expert in your industry, you have to look like a professional.

So, do you look like an expert? Do you look like you have a high IQ in this business? Remember, we're in the real estate business; we're not selling golf courses.

Your presentation should align with your branding. If you market yourself as "legendary, results-driven, and high-class," your image should reflect that. Consumers expect consistency between your branding and how you present yourself in person.

Here's another angle: You do not want to look like your consumer; you want to look like the expert. I find that most agents make the mistake of thinking they need to mirror their client. The problem with that is, the client doesn't value you as an expert when you're mirroring them. You have to come up a step ahead of them.

Someone once said to me, "You don't dress for the position you have. You dress for the position you want." So do you want to be a million-dollar commission earner? Do you want to be a successful real estate agent? Are you dressing for that position? This is a part of the total package of being an agent with a high *Real Estate IQ.*

It's also important to note that your brand goes beyond how you dress and speak. Successful agents are known for getting results quickly and creating a sense of urgency. A strong brand should reflect these attributes, making clients feel they're working with someone who delivers fast and efficiently.

You do not want to look like your consumer; you want to look like the expert.

Everywhere you go—whether at a networking event, a restaurant, or even just running errands—you could meet your next client. Your brand doesn't turn off when you leave the office.

Let's recap: to be a high-IQ, top-producing agent, you need to:

- define your expertise and master it;
- stay informed about your market, from properties to community development;
- present yourself professionally to match your brand; and
- operate with urgency and confidence.

Being an expert isn't just about what you know—it's about how you show up, present yourself, and execute.

Real Estate IQ Assessment

Section 1: Identifying Your Expertise

1. Which real estate niche do you specialize in? *(Check all that apply)*

- Land and Farmland

- Golf Course Communities

- Beachfront Properties

- Luxury Homes

- New Construction

- Single-Family Homes

- Condos (High-rise, Riverfront, Golf Course, etc.)

- Commercial Real Estate

- Investment Properties

- Other: _____

2. How do you justify your expertise in this niche? *(Check all that apply)*

- I have actively studied this market for years.

- I consistently sell properties in this category.

- I have in-depth knowledge of trends, pricing, and opportunities.

- I can confidently answer detailed client questions without Googling.

- I regularly network with professionals in this market (e.g., builders, developers, membership directors).

- I attend community events, commission meetings, or industry seminars related to this niche.

3. Can you confidently answer these detailed questions in your niche without research? *(If applicable to your niche, check all that apply)*

- What are the top golf courses in my market, their designers, and their membership structures?

- Which new construction communities have available inventory, and what incentives do they offer?

- What is the average price per square foot for properties in my niche?

- Which upcoming developments could impact property values?

- How do HOA fees compare across different communities in my area?

- What are the pros and cons of different financing options in my niche?

If you checked fewer than three, consider deepening your knowledge in this area.

Section 2: Market Awareness & Community Expertise

4. How well do you know your market? *(Rate yourself on a scale of 1-5, with 1 being "not at all" and 5 being "expert level.")*

- Local school ratings and new school developments: [1-2-3-4-5]

- New businesses, restaurants, and shopping centers opening soon: [1-2-3-4-5]

- Road expansions and city planning that could impact property values: [1-2-3-4-5]

- Growth trends and gentrification areas in my city: [1-2-3-4-5]

- Future zoning changes or commercial development plans: [1-2-3-4-5]

If you rated any category below a 3, consider attending city commission meetings, networking with developers, or studying local trends.

Section 3: Branding & Professionalism

5. Do you project the image of an expert? *(Check all that apply)*

- I dress professionally and appropriately for my clientele.

- My personal branding (social media, website, and marketing) aligns with my expertise.

- I maintain an authoritative yet approachable presence online and in person.

- My clients describe me as knowledgeable, confident, and results-driven.

- I regularly post market updates and insights to establish credibility.

- I have received referrals because of my perceived expertise.

If you checked fewer than three, focus on improving your branding and confidence.

Section 4: *Real Estate IQ* Growth Plan

6. What are your next steps to improve your *Real Estate IQ*? (*Check all that apply*)

- Attend a city commission or planning meeting.

- Shadow an expert in my niche to deepen my understanding.

- Visit three to five communities or developments I haven't explored yet.

- Take a course or certification in my specialty.

- Improve my branding and personal image to align with my expertise.

- Create a content plan to share valuable insights on social media.

- Set up meetings with industry professionals (builders, membership directors, developers).

Commit to at least three of these action items in the next 30 days.

Assessment Results & Final Thoughts

If you scored high in multiple areas → You're well on your way to being a high-IQ real estate professional! Keep refining your expertise and ensuring your branding aligns with your skills.

If you found gaps in your knowledge → Now you know where to focus! Set a plan to build expertise in one key area before branching out further.

If your branding and image need work → Enhance your professionalism! First impressions matter—make sure you present yourself as the expert you are striving to be.

Creating a Winning Strategy for Current Market Conditions

In today's market, where buyers and sellers are moving across the country at unprecedented rates, having trusted agent connections in different cities and states is essential. It's no longer just about your immediate market—it's about having a nationwide (and even global) network of professionals you can confidently refer clients to.

For example, if you're an agent in Texas and a client is relocating from Dallas to Fort Worth—a market you may not cover—you need a reliable referral partner in that area. Referrals are not just a professional courtesy; they are a legitimate income stream. Agents who fail to cultivate these relationships are leaving money on the table.

This is also one of the key reasons why some 100-percent-commission models don't work for every agent—they often lack the community and referral culture that allows agents to share business and build a trusted network. At Call It Closed®, we have deliberately built a culture of collaboration, allowing agents to create strong relationships across the country and, as we expand, even internationally.

Building these relationships requires more than just exchanging business cards at a conference. Attending industry events, engaging with other professionals, and staying active in agent networks ensures that when you need to refer a client, you're sending them to someone you truly trust.

This is crucial because your reputation is tied to every referral you make. If you send a client to an agent who delivers a poor experience, it reflects negatively on you. Think of it like influencer marketing—when an influencer recommends a product and it turns out to be low quality, their credibility takes a hit. The same principle applies in real estate. If I refer a client to another agent and that agent drops the ball, I'm the one who loses trust with the client, making them less likely to refer future business to me.

Clients today are looking for high-quality professionals they can trust, and as an agent, that means being just as selective about who you recommend as you are about who you work with directly. Long-term success isn't just about transactions—it's about curating a network of reliable professionals that clients can count on, whether they're moving across town or across the country.

As we mentioned, real estate used to be deeply personal—buyers would walk into a home, envision where their couch would go, imagine holidays around the dining table, and feel a connection to the space. Decisions were often made based on instinct, emotion, and a sense of belonging. Today, however, data-driven decision-making has taken over.

Clients today are looking for high-quality professionals they can trust.

With so much accessibility to information, buyers are relying less on gut instinct and more on analytics and algorithms to guide their decisions. Instead of standing in a home and picturing their future there, they are checking market trends, price-per-square-foot comparisons, and neighborhood statistics to determine whether a house is a "smart" buy. If the data suggests a property is overpriced or outside of market norms, many buyers will walk away—regardless of how much they love the home.

This shift is reshaping the way real estate agents approach their business. Instead of simply appealing to a buyer's

emotions, agents must now come prepared with hard data
to justify a listing price, a neighborhood's value, or a home's
long-term investment potential. At the same time, it presents
challenges because some factors—such as a home's character,
unique charm, or future potential—can't always be quantified in
a spreadsheet.

How Agents Can Adapt to Data-Driven Clients

Fighting against data isn't an option—the only way to work
with it is to leverage it in negotiations. If a buyer sees data that
suggests a home is overpriced, an agent needs to come in with a
strategy to align pricing with market expectations. If the concern
is neighborhood trends, an agent must guide the client to credible
third-party sources for research while helping them understand
the bigger picture.

For instance, agents are not legally allowed to discuss crime
statistics or school quality due to fair housing regulations.
Instead, they must direct clients to research tools that provide
that information. This ensures that consumers are making
informed decisions without agents violating ethical or legal
boundaries.

Many people end up buying out of necessity rather than
preference, and the data supports this. According to recent
statistics, 23 percent of homebuyers made their purchase because
they had no other choice. Life circumstances—such as job loss,
relocation, family emergencies, or financial hardship—force
individuals and families into the market, often at a time they
wouldn't have chosen otherwise.

I recently worked with a client in this exact situation. He lost his job, and with seven kids to care for, his family had to leave their home and move to Austin, where he had a new job. The problem? They had bought during the COVID market boom, and now they were $200,000 underwater. It was heartbreaking, but it's also a reality that many homeowners face.

I worked with this client and told him he had an option. He could keep the home and rent it out, rather than losing the $200,000. The problem was that their cash was tied up in that house, so they couldn't go buy another home. So their best option was, which is what they ended up doing, was keeping the home and then renting a second smaller home to live in until this house catches up. It was a hard decision for his family to make, but the reality is they had to make the better decision. They had to choose the lesser of two evils, and the best one was keeping the home.

I had an investor say to me one time, "Americans are stupid in the way they think about real estate." And I thought, *Wow! That's very offensive. I'm an American!* He said, "If you look at the ten-year run of a home, it's going to have ebbs and flows, ups and downs. But at the end of the ten years in that run, it's probably going to catch itself. Say the house goes up $100,000, down $100,000, up $100,000, and down $100,000—it will at least level out in those ten years, or maybe even be worth more in the end. So basically there was a season where the average homeowner lived in their home four years and four months. Then it was in seven years and nine months. Now they're predicting that because the 2 percent interest rate, it will be higher than that. But Americans want to move every two years."

I'm a guilty of that myself; but because I'm smart, I've never lost money on a house. I know how to run the two-year "seasons". But the point this investor was making (he was from Germany) is that they think in twenty-year runs and Americans think in two-year runs. So if you think about it and say, *I'm going to keep this house for twenty years*, the market may go up and down fifty times in twenty years; but at the end of those twenty years, it will be worth more. And if you have a renter in there, you can make even more.

This is where you take emotion out the equation. If you do that with every transaction, you can think more logically than you do emotionally. Going back to the story of my client, he has turned his house into a rental to cover his mortgage payment. He can't go buy another house yet because he doesn't have the cash to pay down on the loan. But he can put a renter in here; so in one year, he can go get a mortgage on another house in Texas, where he moved for his new job, and he can show that he has had someone else paying his mortgage for one year.

So his story actually had a good ending. Now he will own two homes that are increasing in value, which is what I begged him to do, instead of just dumping one and losing $200,000. The lesson here is: Don't act on emotion and lose $200,000. Think bigger and hold on longer. When you're in a crisis like that, think ten years instead of two, or even five. Don't go into crisis mode and do something stupid.

I want to speak to the importance of keeping your focus on the families you're putting in the homes you sell. When I say this to agents as I'm training them, they look at me like a deer caught in the headlights because all most of them are thinking about is a salary or a paycheck. The problem with that, of course, is that's what is driving you instead of the emotion of putting a family in a home they will love and enjoy. If you lose sight of the family, you lose sight of the purpose of what you're doing. To me, a home is family. Even if it's just for one person, they are a family. Maybe their family is a cat, but they still have Christmas and Thanksgiving and other life events there.

Even if you're selling the home to an investor, that investor is making money off of a house so they can bring more money back to their family bank account or the family trust. So even if it's an investment property, they may not be personally putting up a Christmas tree in that house, but it's still feeding and funding their personal home.

The bottom line is, you're not selling houses—you're selling homes.

Fear-based decision-making plays a major role in why the market stagnates. Uncertainty—whether from political instability, economic downturns, or global events—causes buyers to hesitate. Rather than investing in real estate, many choose to rent longer, believing it offers more flexibility.

But here's what most people don't realize: renting is often a far greater financial risk than buying.

People feel comforted by the idea that they can walk away from a lease in twelve months, but if they took the time to do the math, they'd see that renting is essentially paying hundreds of thousands of dollars over time with zero return. The long-term financial loss is staggering, yet fear keeps many from committing to homeownership.

The bottom line is, you're not selling houses— you're selling homes.

A client recently asked me, "What if the market goes down and I end up upside down in my home?" It's a common fear, but I always ask: Are you planning on selling in two years, or are you planning on keeping the home?

Going back to my previous story, most homeowners actually stay in their homes much longer than they expect to. Nationally, the average homeowner tenure is thirteen years, though that number varies by market. Even if the market fluctuates in the short term, home values historically recover over time. The ups and downs only matter if you're selling at the wrong time.

If you plan to keep your home for seven, ten, or thirteen years, the day-to-day market changes are irrelevant. The alternative— renting for over a decade—means throwing away money you'll never see again. At least when you're making mortgage payments, you're building equity, paying down your loan, and creating a long-term financial asset.

The Five Biggest Mistakes
Real Estate Professionals
Make During Downturns

A market downturn can cause panic for many real estate professionals, but the ones who stay strategic, maintain consistency, and avoid common pitfalls are the ones who come out ahead. The agents who fail to adapt usually make one (or more) of the following mistakes:

1. They stop doing what made them successful in the first place.

   Many agents scale back their marketing efforts, thinking they should cut costs during a slowdown. For example, if an agent was mailing a monthly market update to a neighborhood but stops because sales are slow, they risk losing visibility. When the market picks up again, they've already been forgotten by potential clients who have moved on to an agent who remained consistent.

   The definition of insanity is doing the same thing over and over again and expecting to achieve different results. However, in real estate, opposite of that can be true as well. If you're successful in this business and you *stop* doing the things that made you successful and go do something else, you're following a path that is the opposite of the pattern of success, and you won't get the same results. When you find the pattern of success, you should keep doing the things you've been doing.

   We've talked about the fact that humans are pattern-oriented people; we're creatures of habit who are accustomed to following a specific routine—and that includes the routines we've established that have formed the patterns that have led to our success, So the moment we break the routines that have made us successful agents, we actually break the pattern of success in our business.

The moment we break the routines that have made us successful agents, we actually break the pattern of success in our business.

For example, let's say you: (1) allow your emotions to drive your business instead of the actual disciplines of success, (2) you haven't brought the right mentors and coaches into your life, and (3) you're doing the wrong things over and over again expecting a different result. That's just ignorance. You're not going to get the results you want.

So the reality is, you don't want to be an ignorant real estate agent. You want to be a growing agent. You want to have a high *Real Estate IQ*. You want to surround yourself with other successful people. You don't want to be driven by your emotions. You want to be success driven. You want to look at yourself in the mirror and ask, *Can I do better?* And the answer is "Yes, we can all do better!"

So, in a downturn, the first thing you need to do is have a gut check to see who you are. You need to recognize that you were successful. Then you have to ask yourself some hard questions:

- *Even though the market has changed, am I in it for the long haul or was I just a blip in the radar?*
- *Was this was just a moment in my life, or is it really my career?*

Then you have to make a decision about what you will do in the downturn. Ask:

- *Am I survivor?*
- *Will I make it?*
- *Will I surround myself with successful people?*
- *Will I find my pattern of success and stick with it?*

2. They disengage from their communities.

Successful agents are embedded in their communities— not just selling homes, but being active participants. During downturns, agents who withdraw from local events, networking groups, or industry associations lose touch with both potential clients and valuable referrals.

Relationships drive real estate, and downturns are when relationships matter most.

When you disengage from your community, you become the disappearing agent—the agent who is no longer there—and people start assuming that you changed careers and you're no longer a professional in the industry. Yes, many agents do sometimes have a side hustle, but they don't need to let it become public knowledge that they're doing it. They can actually stay plugged into their communities at the same time.

In fact, during downturn markets, you have the time to plug into more community events. When the market's on fire, you don't have time to plan a yard sale for your community, but when the market's down, you do. So instead of unplugging, you should be plugging in more and getting your face out more. Why would you not be doing more if you're not selling as many houses and you have more time?

3. They speak negatively about the market.
The way an agent talks about the market affects both their mindset and their business. If an agent continuously complains about how bad the economy is or how difficult the market has become, they create a negative perception that drives clients away. Buyers and sellers don't want to work with someone who lacks confidence—they want an agent who offers solutions, stability, and perspective.

I call these people Eeyore (like the depressed donkey in the Winnie the Pooh books) real estate agents. What

happens is Eeyores attract other Eeyores, and they create
clubs of negativity, versus getting around people who are
surrounded by quality mentors. No one wants "woe-is-me"
real estate agents, and people don't want to work with
negative people. It's just a fact of life. I don't care what
industry you're in, people in that industry don't want to
work with negative people. They want to feel happy, They
want to feel excited. They want to feel joy. Homebuyers
want to feel excited about bringing their newborn baby
home to the new house they just bought. They want to feel
excited about the sign on the lawn with their kid's picture
on it when they're graduating—those signs everyone
does with "Class of 2025 graduate." These are the kinds
of things they have close in their heart and are excited
about. They're not thinking, *Oh, the economy's up* or *The
economy's down.* They're excited about getting that photo
on their front lawn of their house, And if you're not excited
about the photo and you're just thinking about the market
being down—STOP! Stop thinking about what the
market's doing and think about what the family is doing.

As an agent in a downturn market, you determine
your success. You have to separate family and business.
You don't have to be in a crisis in every slow market.
The market is going to have ups and downs. Everything
that rises, falls; and everything that falls is going to rise.
It's just a season. If you look at the big picture of my
twenty-three-year career, there have been several ups
and downs in the market. The reality is, just like you, I
have to stay steady; if I don't, my clients will not feel my
steadiness in the market.

So you have to constantly be judging yourself. *Am I being an Eeyore? Am I being a negative person in my market? Am I giving off the vibe that I'm concerned or that the market's in crisis?* Again, you have to remember the kids standing on the front lawn taking the picture. They're not thinking about what the house value is. They're thinking about their family, and that's what you have to think about to keep that negative thought process at bay. Don't forget that people always need a home, which is my next point.

Stop thinking about what the market's doing and think about what the family is doing.

4. They forget that people always need a home.
   No matter what is happening in the economy—whether interest rates are high, inflation is rising, or there is economic uncertainty—people still need a place to live. Homes will always be bought and sold, even in challenging times. Agents who focus on meeting people's needs rather than reacting to market conditions will continue to do business, regardless of external circumstances.

The reality is, you cannot forget that people need homes and that you can't judge people's lives through their families. What they do behind the four walls of their home is sacred. It's beautiful. It's beautiful for them, it's beautiful for their lives, and it's even beautiful for their pets. You can't lose sight of the beauty of families. Sometimes you may be thinking about your own family and your own home. Maybe you're not making as much money as the family you've sold a home to. You have to let go of that and be willing as an agent to adjust your lifestyle to your own budget if you're in a down market, rather than overspending on your credit cards. You can't just think, *I had a good year two years ago, and I'm going to do it again.* Well, until you do it again, you have to adjust.

I remember when the market went down years ago, and I had made a million dollars the year before. Then the next year, I made almost no money. I think I made a million and spent a million in the same year. (I think it should be illegal for someone in their twenties to make a million dollars.) I was so stupid! I had overspent on all my credit cards. I nearly went bankrupt. My car got repossessed the next year. It was awful! And it was because I didn't have anyone in my ear saying, "Hey, you're not going to make the same money every single year." That's when Chad said, "We're doing life differently, and we are going to live on a budget, no matter the ebbs and flows of this business." And that's what we did. We changed our lives, and that was beautiful. That doesn't mean we don't reward our success at times, but it does mean we don't go to the extreme in rewarding ourselves.

I lost a ton of money in that downturn. But the reality is, it taught me a life lesson for the future of ebbs and flows. Even as I was going through that in my own life and business, I couldn't allow my financial crisis to become my client's crisis. I had to keep my focus on my clients and their homes because they weren't in crisis. They were just trying to take pictures of their graduating child in their front lawn or of their new puppy running across that front lawn.

I told you my story. What will your story be?

5. They don't embrace adaptability.

The most successful real estate professionals understand that markets go through cycles. Instead of resisting change, they adjust their strategies, refine their skills, and look for new opportunities. For example, if traditional marketing isn't generating leads, an adaptable agent might shift their focus to social media engagement, digital advertising, or video marketing. If buyers are hesitant, a proactive agent will educate them on creative financing options, such as interest rate buy-downs or seller concessions.

There's a trend that's going around right now of people saying the AI agent will take over and roll over every other agent if they don't adapt to AI. I believe that is a potentially dangerous statement. I do believe AI is a game changer for us as real estate agents, but I don't believe it's going to change the front-facing feel of the agent. I use AI; but the reality is, when a consumer is buying a house, they don't want to buy it with a bot. They want to buy it with a human.

That being said, as a real estate agent, you have to be adaptable to using the tools you need to help you succeed. Using AI or ChatGPT to communicate; to write your listing presentations; to list your photos, descriptions, etc. is wonderful just to make your time more manageable. In fact, if you do not adapt, you'll be behind the times; and you will do fewer transactions than the agents who are using AI. If you're not willing to be changeable, you will be the "sinking Sears." You will be "sitting in the Titanic."

Our industry is moving fast, and you have to be adaptable and stay in the flow. I was on the road off and on for the last couple of months, and I had not shown a house in several weeks. (I'm a buyer's agent.) When I got back in town, I thought, *I have to get my boots on the street so I don't lose my pattern—my routine.* It had only been a few weeks, but I find that you can sometimes lose the way you do things, and you have to learn them again. Even though I've been doing this for twenty-three years, I still felt nervous going to show a house when I got back, and it was a $500,000 house. But I did it because I was determined to put my feet on the ground and not lose my pattern.

I think, as an agent, you have to keep your finger on the pulse of what you're doing. Even in a down market when you don't have houses to show or sell, you have to stay engaged in what's happening, both in the nation's economy and in the economy of your market. The Texas market is different than California, California is different than Florida, and Florida is different than Georgia. You have to keep your finger on whatever is happening in the area you're working in.

And how do you do that? By talking to your local people. Right? Don't forget your relationships with bankers, jewelry store owners, mortgage lenders, car dealership owners, art dealers, farmers, and all the people. Get out there and find out what's happening. Maintain those relationships. Those are the backbone of your business.

Waiting for the old market to return is a losing strategy. What will never change is the fact that the market will always change; it will always shift. The economy will always be changing. The interest rate will always be changing. You have to make sure you are keeping up with change, keeping up with technology, keeping up with what your consumers are reading. You have to adapt.

The Danger of Poor Financial Management in Real Estate

One of the biggest reasons real estate agents struggle—especially during slow markets—is poor financial management. The nature of real estate means inconsistent income. Some months, an agent might close multiple deals and make $25,000 or more, while other months they may have no closings at all. The mistake many agents make is spending as if their commissions will be consistent every month, failing to budget, save, and reinvest in their business.

I often compare it to running a store. Imagine you own a knitting shop and you just sold all your yarn. If you spent every penny of that income, how will you afford to restock your shelves? Many agents don't think of their business this way. They spend everything they earn, without setting aside money for marketing, business growth, or future expenses.

The best agents treat their finances like a business, not a paycheck.

The best agents treat their finances like a business, not a paycheck. One of the best ways to do this is to create a personal commission split, just like a brokerage would. For example:

- Ten percent of every commission should go directly into marketing to keep generating new business.

- A percentage should be set aside for savings, for both personal security and reinvesting in your business.

- Taxes must be accounted for, so there are no surprises at the end of the year.

- An emergency fund should cover unexpected expenses—car repairs, medical bills, or slow months in the market.

- The remaining amount should be the agent's take-home pay, which should be spent based on a reasonable, sustainable budget.

- Most agents don't follow this structure, which is why they end up on what we call the "rollercoaster of finances"—one month they're rich, the next month they're broke. This instability is why many agents don't survive long-term in real estate.

Beyond personal financial security, agents who fail to budget can actually harm their clients. When an agent is struggling financially, their decision-making can become compromised.

For example, let's say an agent is working with a buyer who isn't in a rush. The buyer wants to take their time and find the perfect home. However, the agent needs a paycheck immediately. Instead of prioritizing the client's best interests, the agent may push them to settle for a home that isn't quite right, just to close a deal faster.

That's why financial responsibility isn't just about personal survival—it's about ensuring agents can operate with integrity and always put their clients first.

An agent who is not desperate for a commission check can take the time to listen, strategize, and guide their clients toward the best long-term decision, rather than pushing them into a sale just to make ends meet.

Why Waiting for the Old Market to Return Is a Losing Strategy

Many real estate professionals are holding onto the hope that the market will return to what it once was, but that's a losing strategy. The reality is that the old market isn't coming back—and neither are the conditions that came with it.

We are never going back to a time when Sears dominated retail, when people shopped without using the internet, or when real estate agents relied on a black book of listings and a Rolodex of contacts sitting on their desks. Just as Amazon changed retail forever, the way people buy and sell homes has permanently evolved.

The biggest mistake an agent, investor, or broker can make is to stand still and wait for past conditions to return. The market is always moving—you can either ride the wave, create the wave, or get left behind chasing it. The most successful professionals are the ones who stay ahead of the next shift, rather than waiting for history to repeat itself.

The COVID-era real estate market—with 2 percent mortgage rates and record-low inventory—was a fluke in the system. It was an anomaly driven by global events, government stimulus, and unique financial conditions that are unlikely to ever happen again. Agents and buyers who are waiting for those conditions to return will miss out on real opportunities in the present market.

What Will Never Change in Real Estate

While technology, data, and consumer habits will continue to evolve, one thing will always remain true: people crave connection.

Consumers will always need to feel heard, valued, and understood when making a decision as big as buying or selling a home. The human element of real estate will never go away, even as technology changes the way agents find clients, present deals, and negotiate transactions.

The key to long-term success in real estate is mastering both sides—leveraging modern tools and trends while maintaining the personal connection that makes people trust and choose you over someone else.

Some agents will adapt and thrive, while others will hold onto outdated methods and fall behind. The professionals who embrace change, stay informed, and pivot when necessary will always have a competitive edge.

Waiting for the market to "return to normal" is not a strategy—it's an excuse to stay stagnant. The market will never return to what it was. It will continue to evolve, and those who evolve with it will be the ones who win. No matter what the market is doing, people still need homes.

PART IV: THE PATH
TO GETTING THERE

THE 7 RESIDENTIAL
REAL ESTATE
MUST KNOWS
(ACTIONABLE TACTICS)

A re you hungry? Are you ready to be a "wow" real estate agent?

Are you willing to take the assessment and see where you honestly stand as a real estate agent and make changes in your life? If you're not, please don't read any further.

I dare you to find out who you are! Do you even know? How confident are you? Are you a risk taker? Or do you always stay behind the line?

After being in this business for twenty-three years and selling hundreds of millions of dollars worth of properties, I have mastered most of the concepts of real estate, but it hasn't been because of me. It's been because of the people I've surrounded myself with who have taught me these things. For example, the Tony Jearys of the world have taught me another level of business. That includes the man who owns the patent for bottled water, who is one of my clients. He gets paid six cents for every case of water sold in the world. It also includes another of my clients, the person who owns the patent for the coating that's put on pills to make them easier to swallow. They're all geniuses, and I've learned so much from them.

I'm a real risk taker. I'm constantly asking my clients, "What am I not seeing? What are my blind spots?" And I'm always asking that of successful business people as well. A lot of people don't want to ask those kinds of questions. I'm the kind of person who will say, "You're not my friend" if I have toilet paper hanging down the back of my pants and you don't tell me about it, I'm always asking smart people if there is something on my backside in business that I don't see. I believe that's the reason I can say these things to you, because I've surrounded myself with people who have gone places I've never gone and have accomplished things I've never accomplished. I've let these people speak into my life at a very high level, and I receive it, even though at times it's like a fire saw. I once asked one of my clients, the guy who ran the group of 77 lobbyists that invested hundreds of millions of dollars in the market across the country, "How can I do business better?" I was managing all their assets in the state of Florida. And he said, "You don't answer your phone fast enough. Your voicemail should say (this)." And I mean, he gave it to me.

I would bet that few of you agents who are reading this book have ever asked your clients, "How can I serve you better? What could I have done better?" Most of you may not even want to know the answer because deep down you probably already know it.

The most successful real estate professionals never stop learning. They stay ahead.

How? I believe one answer is to block time in your schedule to learn about new things, like new technology, for example. If you're like me, you probably have a constant barrage of calls from technology companies wanting to sell you new technology. It's so important to stay abreast of what's out there. So we have to constantly be filtering those calls and taking time in our business plan to actually be learning about the new technology that's available. Right now, for example there's a new software program in America called ISAs that can tell you when a person has a high level chance of selling their home. They actually call those people and try to get them to sell their home, and they will even book the appointment for you. I would never have known about that if I hadn't scheduled part of my business plan to constantly be studying new current technology.

I also have to time block understanding consumer behavior. That involves asking my consumers questions. If you don't ask questions, you're never going to get answers. You have to write questions you really want the answers to. But it's not just my personal clients I ask. When I'm at a restaurant, I also ask the waitperson questions. I'm asking questions to many people I know because I want to know what they're feeling, what their emotion is. It's like when you're driving—have you ever wondered, *Where are all these people going? And how did they get here?* I do, all the time. I want to know the answers to those types of questions wherever I go. "Where are you going in life?" "How did you get here?" And it's because I want to know what the consumer mind is.

Market trends are something else I block time for, so that I'm looking at the market trends in my particular market every single day. I have it on my hot sheet. Today we had 429 price decreases in a single day. That's not good. We had 133 new listings, and only 75 sold. That's awful. That's not a good day. I time blook it to look at it every day, usually three times a day. As you can see by the numbers right now, we're in a buyer's market in my area, which covers Naples, Fort Myers, Lehigh, and all the surrounding subdivisions. You have to do a market watch for your state, your region, and your territory; and you have to watch it daily because it can flip tomorrow.

Now, an agent with a low *Real Estate Agent IQ* wouldn't know to do this until someone taught them or they gained life experience as an agent. I was talking to an agent within the last two years, and I said something like, "Oh my gosh, the market trend! Can you believe it?" And they said, "What are you talking about?" I thought, *Wow! You shouldn't even be selling real estate.*

And how are you giving prices to a seller if you don't know the market?

In order to learn continuously, you have to time block, pay attention to, and study these things daily. And again, putting successful leaders around you matters. You cannot work at just some brand box. Brokers and owners who have never even been successful real estate agents but just opened a brokerage firm or bought a franchise often don't really even understand something as important as market watch.

These seven must-know tips have been created in the hopes that you will allow a business person who has had a high level of success to speak into your life.

1. Mastering Market Analysis - Interpreting economic trends and forecasting market movements.

The reality is that many professionals resist change. They fall into comfortable routines—whether it's in their marketing, client interactions, or the way they engage with their communities. While consistency is valuable, stagnation is dangerous.

We are, by nature, patterned people. We wake up and follow the same routines—whether it's making coffee, reading, working out, or skipping workouts. We do what feels familiar. This same pattern-driven behavior exists in business. Agents find marketing strategies that work and stick to them. They rely on old habits, even when the market is shifting. But when the industry moves forward and they remain stuck in the past, their success begins to dwindle.

The best agents ask themselves tough questions, such as:

- *Am I evolving with my industry, or am I stuck in outdated methods?*

- *Is my approach still effective, or am I just doing what's comfortable?*

- *Am I operating in a way that serves my clients' best interests, or am I only serving my own convenience?*

The best agents don't just ask what's working for them today—they ask, What will work for my clients tomorrow?

The most successful real estate professionals never stop learning. They stay ahead of:

- **Technology:** Understanding how AI, big data, and predictive analytics impact the market.

- **Consumer Behavior:** Knowing where buyers and sellers are looking, what they expect, and how they make decisions.

- **Market Trends:** Staying informed on home values, interest rates, and economic factors that affect real estate.

By continuously educating themselves, agents position themselves as leaders in the industry. They don't just react to change—they anticipate it.

The best agents don't just ask what's working for them today— they ask, *What will work for my clients tomorrow?*

2. Building a Digital Presence - Leveraging SEO, social media, and email marketing.

When transactions slow down, many agents panic and take their foot off the gas, believing that slashing expenses—especially branding and advertising—will help them survive. However, this strategy often has the opposite effect. **If you disappear from the market, consumers assume you are out of business.** If you have built a well-recognized personal brand, you have **top-of-mind awareness**, meaning that when buyers or sellers are ready to transact, you're the first person they think of. But if you pull back on marketing when the market slows, you become invisible. And once the market recovers, **it's too late to regain the ground you lost**—your competitors who maintained visibility will have already captured that business.

Successful agents and brokers **budget for marketing year-round**—not just in strong markets, but also in downturns. To truly recession-proof your business, you need to think like a business owner.

- **Always have a marketing budget set aside for at least one year.** This ensures you can continue promoting yourself even when transactions slow down.

- **Keep a percentage of your commission specifically for branding.** The best agents reinvest in themselves and their brand, rather than relying on a brokerage to handle marketing.

- **Remain consistent across all platforms.** Social media, email campaigns, local advertising, and networking events should remain active no matter what the market is doing.

A well-established **brand is recession-proof** because it communicates **trust, consistency, and expertise.** Consumers want to work with agents they perceive as **successful, stable, and knowledgeable**. If you suddenly stop advertising, people will assume:

- you left the business;
- you're struggling and no longer an expert; or
- you're a part-time agent who isn't fully committed.

Many real estate agents misunderstand what branding truly means. They assume it's about their brokerage or the company they work for, but in reality, their personal brand is what makes them stand out. Clients don't just hire an agent because of the brokerage name—they hire them because of their expertise, personality, and the experience they provide.

A strong personal brand isn't just about marketing—it's about establishing trust, recognition, and connection in a highly competitive digital world. Buyers and sellers are inviting agents into their homes, trusting them with one of the biggest financial decisions of their lives. They want to know who they're working with, what makes them different, and why they should trust them over the thousands of other agents in the market.

When I was developing my brand, my PR company conducted interviews with my past real estate clients, friends, and family to uncover the most memorable things about me. I expected to hear about my expertise, negotiation skills, or market knowledge. Instead, across the board, people mentioned my bold, fun shoes. They associated me with my signature red-bottom heels—a detail I had never thought to include in my branding. That realization was eye-opening, but it also shows the value of having fun with your branding. Branding should be fun! Thank goodness, they also said I was legendary and unforgettable, and that I was aggressive and get results quickly.

Branding isn't just about expertise—it's also about personality. People connect with agents on a human level before they ever choose to work with them professionally.

Can an Independent Agent Maintain Their Individuality While Working Under a Company?

A common concern for independent agents joining a brokerage is whether they can still build their personal brand. The answer is absolutely—but only if they work for a company that allows and encourages individuality.

Think about Sears™, a once-dominant retail giant. They sold hundreds of brands under their umbrella, but consumers only recognized the Sears name. This is the same model that some traditional brokerages operate under—they want you to blend into their brand rather than stand out as your own.

But today, consumers choose an agent, not a brokerage. Studies consistently show that buyers and sellers don't pick their agent based on the company they work for—they choose them based on trust, personal connection, and reputation. That's why it's critical for agents to build a brand that is uniquely their own.

At Call It Closed®, we've created a model that allows agents to leverage the power of a brokerage while maintaining their own identity. You get the benefits of a national brand, a supportive network, and shared resources—but you're still building a name for yourself, not just the company.

New agents often think they need to lean on the brokerage name for credibility.

As a result, they spend their hard-earned money on commission splits and fees to a brokerage or brand that ultimately does not provide them with a return on that investment.

I often use this analogy when speaking to agents: Imagine walking into a steakhouse—let's say Ruth's Chris™—and ordering a filet mignon. But when your plate arrives, you're served chopped liver, yet the restaurant still demands the full filet mignon price. Would you ever pay for something that didn't meet your expectations? Of course not! But in real estate, many agents do just that—they hand over thousands of dollars in commission splits to a brand that doesn't actually generate their business or provide the value they expect.

Many brokerages prey on new agents' lack of experience by marketing themselves as the key to success. The reality? Clients don't hire the brand—they hire the agent. Studies consistently show that homebuyers and sellers choose an agent based on relationships, trust, and personal reputation, not the brokerage name on the sign.

There are major real estate brands that deliberately target new agents because they understand one critical fact: 87 out of 100 new agents will leave the industry within three years. These companies structure their entire business model around capturing commission splits from an agent's sphere of influence before that agent inevitably exits the industry.

Here's how it works: A new agent joins a well-known brokerage, believing the brand name will generate business for them. The agent naturally sells homes to friends, family, neighbors, and personal connections—not because of the brokerage, but because of their existing relationships. The brokerage keeps 20-30% (or more) of the agent's commissions on those first 4-10 transactions. After exhausting their sphere of influence, the agent struggles to generate new business because they were never properly trained in lead generation, branding, or marketing. Eventually, they leave the industry without ever building a sustainable, long-term business—but the brokerage has already profited from their early deals.

This model is not designed to make agents successful in the long run—it's designed to capitalize on their personal networks before they fail out of the business.

Instead of handing over $15,000 - $20,000 (or more) per year in commission splits to a brokerage that offers little in return, agents should use that money to build their own brand. If that same agent took their commissions and reinvested into personal branding, lead generation tools, and education, they would have a profitable, independent business that doesn't rely on a brokerage's logo to attract clients.

Agents who succeed long-term understand that the value they bring to the table is their expertise, market knowledge, and ability to serve clients—not the name on their business card.

Experienced agents—those who have been in the industry five or more years—already see through this model and refuse to give away their commissions to a brand that doesn't deliver results. This is why, in many metro areas, the largest and most successful brokerages are shifting to 100-percent commission models.

However, most 100-percent commission brokerages lack the tools, systems, and support that traditional big-box brokerages provide. This is why a modern brokerage model must combine the best of both worlds—allowing agents to keep their commissions while providing cutting-edge tools, marketing, and education.

No matter which brokerage an agent chooses, one thing remains true: They must be in control of their business. New agents need to protect their earnings and invest in themselves first. Instead of giving away a percentage of their income to a brokerage that adds no direct value, they should use that money to build a foundation for long-term success.

Winning Negotiation Tactics – Understanding when to push and when to compromise. One of the most important skills in real estate is negotiation, but many agents sabotage their own deals because they let emotion take over. You cannot be both a strong negotiator and an overly emotional agent—the two don't mix.

Why Emotional Agents Lose Deals

Many agents get emotionally attached to the transaction—whether it's because:

- they're desperate for the commission check and start chasing the deal out of personal financial stress;

- they get too wrapped up in their client's emotions, mirroring their frustration, excitement, or anxiety; or

- they react emotionally to unprofessional agents on the other side of the transaction, escalating conflict instead of managing it.

The moment you let emotions drive your negotiations, you lose your expertise. You stop thinking strategically; you stop seeing the big picture; and, ultimately, you weaken your ability to close the best possible deal for your client.

> Winning strategies for negotiations start with mindset. If you don't see yourself as a winner or an expert, you'll close fewer deals. Confidence is key, and it comes from knowledge. If you don't understand the market or the specifics of a deal, your confidence will suffer. More than 50 percent of negotiation success comes from knowing the market inside and out and communicating that knowledge clearly to the other party.

The Power of Staying Neutral in Negotiations

Great negotiators are:

Steady – They don't react emotionally to challenges or tense situations.

Neutral – They detach from personal feelings and focus on facts, strategy, and outcomes.

Calm – Even when things get tense, they maintain composure and professionalism.

Peacekeepers – They set the tone of the deal, ensuring that emotions don't derail progress.

When you remain level-headed and neutral, your client feels that stability. They mirror your confidence.

When you remain level-headed and neutral, your client feels that stability. They mirror your confidence. If you're calm, they stay calm. If you panic, they panic. A smooth negotiation leads to a better experience for the client and, ultimately, more referrals for you.

Handling Difficult Negotiations and Emotional Counterparts

In every transaction, there will be moments where emotions run high—whether it's a stressed-out buyer, a panicked seller, or a difficult agent on the other side.

If you engage emotionally, you lose control of the deal.

If you stay neutral and professional, you control the deal.

Throughout my career, I've encountered situations where another agent becomes overly aggressive, emotional, or even belligerent during a transaction. Some agents allow their frustration—whether over a low offer, a deal going sideways, or their personal expectations—to spill into unprofessional behavior, resorting to yelling, cursing, or making unreasonable demands.

When faced with this type of behavior, I immediately establish boundaries. If an agent starts raising their voice or using inappropriate language, I firmly interrupt and say:

"Excuse me, I'm not sure how you typically conduct business, but in my professional practice, I do not engage in conversations that involve yelling or inappropriate language. If we need to discuss this deal, we need to do so in a professional and respectful manner. If you need to take a few minutes to collect yourself, that's completely fine, and I'm happy to continue this conversation when you're ready to communicate professionally."

Most of the time, this simple statement forces the agent to reset their approach. However, if they continue their outburst or refuse to engage professionally, I end the call and send a text message:

"When you're ready to have a calm, professional discussion about this transaction, please feel free to call me back."

This strategy serves two purposes: it protects my professionalism and prevents unnecessary escalation. No productive conversation can happen when someone is shouting. If an agent refuses to adjust their behavior after this approach, I escalate the matter by contacting their broker and requesting that they intervene before any further discussion takes place.

Maintaining professionalism in real estate is critical—not just for personal reputation, but for the success of the transaction itself. Transactions involve multiple parties, and the ability to remain composed under pressure is what separates **true professionals from those who let emotions dictate their actions**. I have found that taking control of these conversations and setting a clear expectation for professionalism has significantly improved my ability to navigate difficult negotiations while maintaining respect and control in every situation.

Mastering Negotiation = Mastering Emotional Control

If you want to win more deals, protect your clients' interests, and build a strong reputation, you must master emotional control in negotiations.

One of the keys here is recognizing that the client is having an emotional reaction and verbalizing to the client that they're having the normal emotional highs and lows that people have with the transaction. But at the same time, you need to leverage your stability to let them feel secure. You never want to say to a client, "Hey, you're having an emotional breakdown." You want to respond in a gentle manner, saying something like, "I hear what you're saying. I understand this is extremely stressful." You want to let them know you care and that you know it matters. You can't mirror their emotions. You have to speak in a tone that's steady, calm, cool, collected, and confident.

Detach from personal financial pressure

If you're negotiating from a place of desperation, you've already lost.

Don't mirror your client's emotions. Your job is to guide them, not match their stress or excitement.

Stay steady, neutral, and professional—even when others aren't.

The best negotiators are calm, calculated, and strategic. They don't let emotions cloud their judgment. If you can stay grounded while everyone else is reacting emotionally, you will win more deals, earn more referrals, and elevate your entire career.

3. Leveraging Technology - AI, CRM tools, and automation strategies.

One of the biggest challenges in real estate is that agents try to be all things to all people. They want to be the negotiator, the marketer, the communicator, the photographer, the CRM expert, and the transaction coordinator—all at once. But the reality is, you can't do it all and do it well.

Technology exists to support you, yet many agents resist it. They believe they can handle every aspect of their business manually.

However, the most successful agents recognize their limitations and use AI and technology to fill the gaps.

I had a very successful businessman tell me one time that the strongest leaders in business know their strengths; but more importantly, they know their weaknesses, and they know when to employ and bring in support to help them with their weaknesses. So since that time I have lived by that advice. I make it a point to know my strengths, but I also recognize, own, and employ my weaknesses. Employment might be with a CRM technology or with AI Chat GPT, or it could be with coaches or mentors or other people. I don't look at my weaknesses as a fault; I look at them as an opportunity to employ and bring the right tools around me to actually turn my weaknesses into strengths for my business.

We must face the fact that without technology, we risk becoming obsolete. Without it, we cannot fulfill the desires and expectations of our consumers. Prioritizing ourselves over them is not an option—we must always put them first. This mindset drives us to improve our CRA programs, embrace AI chatbots like ChatGPT, and stay ahead of emerging innovations. Every day, we strive to keep an open mind, challenge ourselves, and leverage new technologies to continuously improve.

Why You Need AI & Automation in Your Business

If you're managing twenty-plus active buyers and sellers, it's nearly impossible to

- **remember their personal details**—their kids' names, their pets, their preferences;

- **track their searches**—what homes they're favoriting, their budget changes;

- **stay on top of communication**—responding quickly and effectively;

- **handle marketing and social media**—keeping your brand fresh and relevant; and

- **manage negotiations and contracts**—while also keeping a full client pipeline.

The solution? Use AI and automation to handle what you can't.

How Technology Elevates Your Business

CRM (Customer Relationship Management) Systems – Platforms like Follow Up Boss™, Lofty™, BoomTown™, or KVCore™ help agents stay organized and in constant communication with clients. These systems send automated messages, reminders, and follow-ups, ensuring no client falls through the cracks.

AI-Powered Chatbots & Virtual Assistants – AI can answer inquiries, schedule appointments, and nurture leads, keeping potential buyers engaged before you even pick up the phone.

Automated Email and Text Follow-Ups – Instead of trying to manually keep track of every lead, automation tools send personalized emails and texts, ensuring you stay top-of-mind with minimal effort.

AI-Powered Market Analytics – AI tools can analyze buyer behavior, market trends, and price fluctuations faster than any human can, giving agents a competitive edge in negotiations.

Social Media and Content Automation – Platforms like Canva, Jasper AI, and ChatGPT can help generate engaging content without spending hours brainstorming captions or creating graphics.

If you're not using technology to scale your business, you're already falling behind.

Why Agents Must Embrace Technology

If you're not using technology to scale your business, you're already falling behind. Clients expect quick responses, detailed insights, and personalized service—things that technology can help you provide effortlessly. Clients want to feel like they are the most important ones you have, and technology helps you deliver on that expectation. Obviously, there are only so many hours in a day. If you're currently juggling even 10 clients—or just a handful—you can't always respond instantly to emails and text messages. This is why powerful platforms like a CRM can help you manage these interactions efficiently. Clients want to feel like they are your top priority, and they don't care that you have other clients to juggle. In fact, they'd prefer not to know. It doesn't matter to them. So, as an agent, how can you make each client feel like they are the most important person to you while they're in the middle of the most significant deal of their life? The answer: by leveraging technology.

AI isn't replacing agents—it's empowering them to be more efficient, more responsive, and more effective. The key is recognizing where you need support and using the right tools to elevate your strengths while covering your weaknesses.

4. Diversifying Income Streams - Rentals, property management, coaching, investing.

If you've been in real estate long enough, you've heard agents talk about the rollercoaster of finances—one month they're flush with cash, the next month they're barely scraping by. This boom-and-bust cycle is a common trap, and it's largely due to the transactional mindset that most agents adopt. Instead of focusing on long-term financial stability, many are constantly chasing the next closing, the next deal, the next client—without a plan for creating lasting wealth.

I want to break that thought process off of any agent reading this. You have to learn how to plan for your future; and if you don't consider multiple streams of income, you will always depend on that next transaction. It's good to have the mindset of "next," but you have to expand that to include creating multiple streams of income.

For many agents, their entire income depends on commissions. This means their financial well-being is tied directly to the ebb and flow of the market, which are unpredictable at best. The reality is that the market is never stable—it shifts, slows down, speeds up, and sometimes grinds to a near halt. Without multiple income streams, an agent will always be at the mercy of market conditions they cannot control.

To break free from the commission rollercoaster, agents must shift their mindset. It's not just about wealth; it's about legacy wealth—building sustainable financial security that lasts beyond just the next transaction. Many agents rely on a second household income, typically from a spouse, or on traditional retirement plans like 401(k)s. While those can provide some financial stability, they are often not enough to create true long-term wealth.

One of the most effective ways to maintain financial stability is to set up multiple bank accounts to allocate funds wisely. When I receive 100 percent of my commission, I treat my business like a structured enterprise and split my earnings accordingly. I allocate a minimum of 10 percent toward marketing to ensure I stay visible and continue generating leads. I also maintain a dedicated tax account, setting aside money to avoid surprises when tax season arrives. Living expenses are paid from a separate account, and I prioritize savings and investments in a fourth account to build long-term wealth.

The biggest financial pitfall for real estate agents is treating every good month as the new normal. Just because you have a few high-earning months doesn't mean you can afford to live as if that level of income is guaranteed every month. Many agents fall into the trap of overspending during good months, only to find themselves struggling when the market slows down. This cycle— what we call the "rich-one-month-broke-the-next" mindset— prevents many agents from ever truly achieving financial security in this business.

The most successful real estate professionals don't just sell real estate—they own real estate, invest in companies, and leverage revenue-generating opportunities within the industry.

Instead, agents need to intentionally create additional streams of income that will allow them to prosper in any market. The most successful real estate professionals don't just sell real estate— they own real estate, invest in companies, and leverage revenue-generating opportunities within the industry.

Three Key Income Streams Every Real Estate Professional Should Consider

1. Investing in Real Estate

   Real estate agents spend their days selling properties, yet far too many don't invest in properties themselves. The first step to breaking the cycle of financial uncertainty is building a personal real estate portfolio.

   - Rental properties: Whether commercial or residential, owning rental properties provides consistent monthly income, offering financial stability even when commissions are slow.

   - Fix-and-flips: Buying undervalued properties, renovating them, and reselling for a profit can be a lucrative way to generate additional income.

   - Short-term rentals: Platforms like Airbnb™ and VRBO™ have created new passive income opportunities for real estate professionals who understand market trends.

2. Revenue Share and Referral Programs

   Most real estate professionals—especially the most influential ones in a market—naturally attract other agents. Whether through high-level production, mentorship, networking, or affiliation with a strong brokerage or team, agents influence where others choose to work. However, in traditional brokerages, this influence often goes unrewarded.

Several years ago, Keller Williams introduced a profit-sharing model to incentivize agents for bringing in other producing agents. At the time, this was considered cutting-edge. However, the challenge with profit-sharing is that the profitability of individual offices can vary. If an office generates little or no profit, there's nothing to share—leaving agents without financial benefit.

Modern brokerages, like ours at Call It Closed®, have moved toward a revenue-sharing model instead. Under this system, a percentage or specific amount from each closing is paid directly to the sponsoring agent—not from profits, but from revenue. This ensures that agents receive compensation regardless of the company's profitability, making the potential earnings from these programs significantly more substantial. This referral-based income model gives agents the ability to build passive, long-term revenue streams, earning income even when they're not actively closing deals.

I've personally witnessed this in action. When my husband and I built one of the fastest-growing RE/MAX® franchises in the world in 2012, we didn't "hire" 110 agents—we hired about 30, and the rest followed. That's the power of relationships in this business.

Some agents associate recruiting with negative connotations. However, the reality is that all brokerages—regardless of brand or model—must continually bring in new talent to thrive.

Instead of viewing it as recruiting, think of it as collaboration. Real estate professionals naturally gravitate toward working with colleagues and friends they trust. This doesn't mean sending spam emails, cold-calling agents, or using aggressive tactics— practices that most revenue-sharing brokerages discourage. Instead, the focus should be on referring agents you've personally worked with and who align well with your brokerage's culture.

Today, many brokerages recognize and reward agents for fostering these relationships, providing them with real financial opportunities—not just benefiting the company, but also benefiting the agents who help it grow.

3. Stock and Equity Ownership

Another often-overlooked wealth-building tool is owning stock in the right company and at the right time. (It's often best to invest at the beginning when a company is growing the fastest, as it can possibly yield 20-to-1 returns—but this is not guaranteed, of course.)

- Certain brokerages provide stock incentives, allowing agents to build equity over time simply by doing what they already do—selling homes.

- Being part of a growing company with stock options can be an incredible way to build long-term wealth without additional effort.

- Instead of only relying on commissions, agents can ride the growth of a company and profit from stock appreciation.

This is legacy wealth—the kind of financial security that lasts beyond your next closing, beyond your career, and into your retirement.

6. Perfecting Client Communication - Active listening, handling objections, and persuasion.

One of the biggest complaints from consumers and national reporting agencies is that real estate agents fail to communicate properly. This is a critical weakness in the industry, yet the solution is incredibly simple: answer your phone, return business calls, and communicate proactively.

How One Small Change Increased My Business

Early in my career, I had a high-end investor client who gave me a valuable piece of advice. He told me, "If you would simply update your voicemail every morning and let callers know when they can expect a response, it would make a huge difference."

At the time, I was in one of my busiest seasons, closing 355 transactions in a single year. I decided to implement his advice. Every morning, I recorded a new voicemail that went something like this:

> "Hello, today is [date]. I'm in the office and will be returning all calls between 3 PM and 4 PM. Please leave a message, and I will get back to you within that time. If you need immediate assistance, please send me a text."

That small shift transformed my business. My clients felt confident knowing that their calls were important and that they would get a response by the end of the day. They no longer had to guess whether I had received their message or wonder when I would call back. Communication builds trust, and trust builds business.

Why Agents Struggle with Communication

Many agents avoid communication for these three main reasons:

1. They don't know what to say. If a house isn't selling or there's nothing new on the market, they feel like they have nothing to report.

2. They fear delivering bad news. They avoid telling the truth because they're afraid of losing the client.

3. The third reason is communication itself—or rather, the lack of it. Some agents simply don't like talking to people, or they feel overwhelmed by the constant calls from clients. Their phones might be ringing non-stop. Another possibility is that they're exhausted, burned out from too much interaction, or they just aren't naturally great communicators. In some cases, they may not even see communication as a big deal.

But here's the reality: If you fail to communicate, you will lose the client anyway.

The Role of an Expert Communicator

A true professional is never afraid of the truth. Markets change, inventory fluctuates, and challenges arise. An expert agent knows how to navigate these conversations with confidence.

1. If a home isn't selling, explain why. Show the data, discuss pricing, and strategize solutions.

2. If the market is slow, be honest. Clients respect transparency.

3. If a buyer has no homes to see, educate them. Keep them informed on future listings and strategies.

Being an expert isn't about always having the perfect answer— it's about being willing to communicate clearly, honestly, and consistently.

The Responsibility of the Communicator

One of the most eye-opening lessons I learned in a communication training class was this:

> *"It is the responsibility of the communicator—not the receiver—to ensure the message is understood."*

That concept shifted my entire approach. It's not the client's job to decipher what I'm saying—it's my job to communicate in a way they understand. If my message isn't getting across,

I need to adjust how I'm delivering it. This change happened when I challenged myself to become a better communicator and adjusted the way I interacted, not just with my clients but also with my family, friends, colleagues, and church community. It was an incredible lesson. Changing the way I communicated and taking full responsibility for it was difficult, but once I did, everything improved. I focused on my body language, refined how I delivered messages, and became more intentional with my communication. I began to see a shift in how my clients responded to me—they enjoyed communicating with me more. It was a powerful life lesson that I now apply to all areas of my life.

Communication is Not Optional

If you want to be successful in real estate—or any business—you must be a strong communicator. That means:

1. taking ownership of every conversation;
2. ensuring clarity in every interaction;
3. following up consistently: and
4. communicating even when it's difficult.

There will be days when you don't feel like making that last call, responding to that text, or giving a seller bad news. But communication is not optional. It's a non-negotiable part of this business.

7. Creating a Scalable Business Model – Systems that allow you to grow sustainably.

Scalability isn't just about growth—it's about evolution. A business that refuses to change is a business that will eventually become obsolete. If you're stuck in an outdated mindset, resistant to innovation, or unwilling to recognize emerging trends, you are limiting your own potential and setting yourself up for stagnation.

A perfect example of this is a broker I recently encountered. She firmly believes she can sustain her business using the same traditional model she has relied on for years. While she may be able to maintain her current level of success for a short time, her model has no room for expansion. Why? Because she refuses to evolve. She's unwilling to recognize market shifts, adjust her approach, or acknowledge the blind spots in her strategy.

The truth is, if you are unchangeable, you are unscalable.

This is the same mistake that led to the downfall of once-iconic brands like Sears™, Toys 'R' Us™, and Blockbuster™. These companies dominated their industries for decades, but they became complacent. They clung to outdated business models, ignored changing consumer behavior, and ultimately lost relevance. The result? They were replaced by more adaptable competitors who recognized the future before it arrived.

The truth is, if you are unchangeable, you are unscalable.

Why Business Owners Resist Change

Many business owners resist change because they fear it will impact their profit margins. And yes, innovation often comes with short-term challenges. But the greater risk is staying the same. The longer you hold onto outdated methods, the more you lose in the long run.

If you want to scale your business, you must be willing to:

- recognize industry shifts before they disrupt your business;

- adapt to changing consumer behavior and market demands;

- challenge your current model, even if it means temporary discomfort; and

- take a step back to slingshot forward—sometimes short-term sacrifices lead to long-term growth.

Some people aren't scalable simply because they're unwilling to take a step back to leap forward. They fear change so much that they choose stagnation over innovation. But the businesses that embrace change, innovate, and proactively adjust are the ones that thrive.

BUILDING RELATIONSHIPS TO STRENGTHEN YOUR POSITION

If I've not stressed it enough, in real estate, success is deeply tied to relationships—not just with clients but with community leaders, industry professionals, and key business owners. Too often, agents limit their networking to immediate neighbors or fellow agents, failing to expand their connections beyond the obvious. But the reality is, the more people who know you, recognize you, and engage with you, the stronger your position becomes in your market.

I've spoken about the importance of building relationships with luxury service providers—art dealers, car dealers, and high-end jewelry store owners. These relationships strengthen your position because they connect you with individuals who are likely to buy and sell high-value properties.

For example, I've built relationships with the owners of Porsche, Mercedes, and Ferrari dealerships, as well as the managers of high-end restaurants like Ruth's Chris and Chops. These places are hubs for affluent clientele, and being known in these circles gives you access to potential buyers and sellers who may never look for an agent through traditional methods.

Beyond luxury networks, community events like farmers markets, art galleries, and town gatherings are essential for establishing yourself as a recognizable figure. Your brand is built on visibility and relationships. Being well-connected isn't just about socializing—it's about positioning yourself as a local authority in real estate.

One of the most overlooked ways to strengthen your position is getting involved in city planning and government meetings. In my market, the city's planning manager holds meetings every Tuesday to discuss development projects, infrastructure changes, and future community plans.

Attending these meetings has directly led to some of my biggest transactions because these rooms are filled with builders, developers, and commercial investors—the exact people who shape the future of the real estate market. If you're not in the room, you're missing opportunities that most agents never even know exist.

I once attended a meeting where a major road expansion was announced before it was made public. That expansion instantly increased the value of surrounding properties. Because I was in the know before the news broke, I was able to help investors buy strategically and capitalize on the shift. There were only two real estate agents in that room, yet every home in that area gained immediate value.

This is why being involved at a deeper level matters. Knowing what's happening in your community before the public does strengthens your expertise and gives you an edge over other agents who simply wait for MLS updates.

Whether you're a homeowner or an investor, it's crucial to understand the type of agent you're working with. If you're dealing with an agent who operates at a high level, you could experience tremendous success compared to working with one who lacks that level of expertise and experience.

Many agents believe putting their face on a billboard will establish their brand. But a billboard alone does nothing unless you've already done the groundwork to position yourself as a local expert. Visibility without credibility does not build trust. What truly makes you known in your market is consistently engaging with your community, staying in the know, and being a leader in local events, business, and development. If you want to be seen as the go-to agent, you have to act like one. That means showing up where decisions are made, deals are discussed, and future opportunities are taking shape.

Knowing Your Destination

Real estate success is like using a GPS system. If you don't enter a destination, how will you ever know where you're going? Many agents fail because they have no clear plan or strategy for their position in the market.

If you want to be a leading expert, a sought-after agent, and a community authority, you need a blueprint for how to get there. That means:

- defining the role you want to play in your market;
- strategizing how to position yourself as the expert; and
- committing to consistent networking, market research, and involvement.

Without a clear vision, most agents operate on short-term thinking, chasing deals without a long-term strategy. The most successful agents build their careers by intentionally positioning themselves for future opportunities.

Your success is not just about transactions—it's about positioning yourself as the agent who knows, the agent who leads, and the agent who is always ahead of the market.

Strengthen your relationships, and you strengthen your business.

STAYING AHEAD OF FUTURE MARKET SHIFTS

When it comes to predicting future market shifts, no one has a perfect blueprint. No one can predict with 100 percent certainty what the market will do next. However, there are tremors—early warning signs—that signal shifts before they fully unfold.

For agents and business professionals who truly take their career seriously, staying ahead of these shifts is not optional—it's essential. Understanding market movement requires more than just reacting to downturns; it requires foresight, awareness, and a commitment to continuous learning.

The Difference Between Agents Who React and Agents Who Prepare

Many agents are only focused on the next transaction. They don't look for market shifts unless it's a downturn that directly affects their ability to close deals. But the difference between a transaction-based agent and a market expert is simple:

- A typical agent is just trying to survive in the moment.
- A true professional is anticipating changes before they happen and advising their clients accordingly.

How I Saw the 2006-2007 Crash Before It Happened

During the 2006-2007 market crash, I began to feel the downturn before it was widely recognized. I reached out to 300 investors who owned millions of dollars in real estate and told them, "The crash is coming. Sell. Sell. Sell."

Because of that early warning, I helped liquidate 355 homes in a short period of time—protecting investors from deeper losses. Only two investors ignored the warning and stayed in too long, paying the price.

The reason I saw it coming wasn't because of a crystal ball—it was because I was paying attention. While most agents were focused on the next deal, I was analyzing trends, watching inventory shifts, tracking financing changes, and seeing the bigger picture.

This isn't about bashing other agents—it's about making a clear distinction. Not all agents operate the same way.

For consumers looking to hire an agent, the difference is this:

- A **short-sighted** agent focuses only on closing today's deal.
- A **forward-thinking** agent considers how today's market affects tomorrow's financial outcome.

If I'm representing a client, their long-term success matters to me. I care about:

- how market changes impact their investments;
- what's happening with roads, infrastructure, and commercial developments; and
- what policies or zoning changes could affect home values.

This is why knowledge matters. This is why I take it upon myself to stay ahead of market trends—not just for my own success, but for my clients' well-being. The Bible says, "My people perish for lack of knowledge," and I believe that applies to business just as much as life. Many professionals fail, not because they lack talent, but because they lack awareness. They are disconnected from what's happening beyond their immediate transactions.

In today's world, people often assume they can learn everything from sitting behind a computer screen. They rely solely on digital reports, market charts, and online data. But numbers don't tell the full story.

We are in a digital age, but real estate is still, at its core, a people business.

- You can't fully understand a market from behind a screen.
- You can't anticipate trends if you're not actively engaged with your community.
- You can't truly advise clients if you don't have a deep pulse on market conditions.

Success in real estate requires more than just technical knowledge—it requires relationships, instinct, and experience. To stay ahead, you have to be willing to see beyond today's deal and prepare for tomorrow's reality.

CONCLUSION

THRIVING THROUGH CHANGE: POSITIONING YOURSELF FOR LONG-TERM SUCCESS

The real estate industry is constantly evolving, and as professionals, we are either adapting to the shift or being left behind by it. The agents, brokers, and investors who succeed in this business are those who recognize that market changes are not obstacles—they are opportunities.

Throughout this book, we've explored:

- where the industry has been and the lessons from past market cycles;

- where we are now and how technology, consumer behavior, and economic forces are reshaping real estate;

- where you want to be and how to position yourself as a market leader, trusted advisor, and expert; and

- How to get there by implementing actionable strategies, relationship-building techniques, and business models that ensure long-term success.

The Agents Who Win in a Market Shift

The most successful real estate professionals are not simply selling homes—they are navigating trends, anticipating shifts, and positioning themselves ahead of the curve. They are:

- **Market Experts** – They stay informed about local and national trends, economic shifts, and consumer behaviors that impact real estate.

- **Relationship Builders** – They understand that real estate is a people business. They nurture long-term connections with clients, community leaders, developers, and industry professionals.

- **Problem-Solvers** – When challenges arise, they adapt, pivot, and provide solutions rather than waiting for the market to dictate their success.

- **Masters of Negotiation** – They approach every deal with strategy and emotional control, knowing that a strong negotiator must remain calm and neutral.

- **Technology-Driven Professionals** – They embrace AI, automation, CRM tools, and digital marketing to scale their business and serve their clients more effectively.

- **Financially Savvy Entrepreneurs** – They create multiple income streams through investments, revenue-sharing, rental properties, and passive income opportunities, rather than relying solely on commissions.

Many agents and investors hold onto the past, waiting for the conditions of a previous market cycle to return. But here's the reality:

- The market is never going back to what it was.
- What worked five years ago won't work today.
- The only constant in real estate is change.

Instead of resisting the shift, become the agent, broker, or investor who embraces it. Those who adapt will not only survive the changing market—they will thrive in it. If you take away one key lesson from this book, let it be this: **Your success in real estate**

is not about the market. It's about how you position yourself within it.

The future belongs to those who are willing to evolve.

The question is: **Are you ready?**

ABOUT THE AUTHOR

A visionary leader in the real estate industry, **Aprile Osborne** is renowned for co-founding Call It Closed®, the pioneering cloud-based, 100-percent commission brokerage with a revolutionary revenue-sharing model. With over two decades of experience, Aprile has been at the forefront of transforming the industry, empowering thousands of agents to achieve financial independence.

Recognized as one of the Top Female Leaders in Real Estate, Aprile has been featured on multiple media platforms for her groundbreaking contributions. Her twenty-plus years of experience have consistently driven innovation and success across various markets.

As the leader of one of the fastest growing RE/MAX® franchises, Aprile's exceptional leadership skills have been instrumental in driving growth and achieving outstanding results. With personal sales exceeding $500 million, she is a top-performing sales professional in the country.

Aprile is a sought-after mentor and coach, dedicated to empowering agents to scale their businesses and achieve long-term success. She has been instrumental in developing innovative models that provide agents with autonomy, financial freedom, and the tools they need to thrive.

ABOUT CALL IT CLOSED® (CIC)

CIC is committed to its philosophy—which is to give to others more than they take. The company was formed based upon Aprile and Chad Osborne's history of being (each at different times) the owner of the fastest growing REMAX® franchise in the world and their twenty-year history of dedicated real estate service. They grew to become one of the largest—if not *the* largest—real estate producing agencies in the state of Florida through studying models that would allow realtors who followed the model to pull ahead and win. They created a company, Call It Closed® (CIC), based on those best practices, with the foundation being a 100-percent-commission model.

Please scan this QR code and take a look at their video, and/or please visit callitclosed.com to learn more about their company. And if this book was given to you by a CIC agent who may have asked you to consider joining CIC, please, by all means, honor that connection. Reach back out to that person and have them lead you through the process of seeing if CIC is the right brokerage firm for you. If they are, please join us, and even one day use this book as a recruiting tool for yourself. We believe CIC is one of the best brokerage options in the world today. There are other great brokerage options out there; pick the one that's best for you and has the best timing for you to take advantage of winning for your particular circumstances.

The 7 Must-Knows Self-Assessment

1. Mastering Market Analysis	F	D	C	B	A
How well do you track and anticipate shifts in market trends, interest rates, and consumer behavior? **My Rating:**	Rarely tracks market trends or economic factors.	Occasionally reviews trends but does not apply them to strategy.	Reviews market trends and applies insights inconsistently.	Regularly analyzes market data and adjusts strategies accordingly.	Consistently forec trends and adapts proactively.

2. Building a Digital Presence	F	D	C	B	A
How consistent and strategic is your personal brand across digital platforms? **My Rating:**	No digital presence or brand strategy.	Occasionally posts but lacks consistency and strategy.	Active but engagement and branding are weak.	Maintains a strong, consistent brand across platforms.	Recognized as a to industry brand wit high engagement visibility.

3. Winning Negotiation Tactics	F	D	C	B	A
How well do you manage emotional control and strategic positioning during negotiations? **My Rating:**	Easily emotional, reactive, and struggles to stay composed.	Sometimes loses emotional control or concedes too easily.	Maintains composure but could improve strategic leverage.	Stays calm and negotiates effectively most of the time.	Expert at controllir emotions and maximizing negotiation outcomes.

4. Leveraging Technology	F	D	C	B	A
How effectively do you use technology to streamline and scale your business? **My Rating:**	Avoids technology or has no system in place.	Uses basic tools but lacks integration or automation.	Utilizes some tech but could optimize usage.	Leverages CRM, AI, and automation effectively.	Uses cutting-edge technology for maximum efficien and scalability.